Why Be a Catholic?

WHY BE A CATHOLIC?

248.842

Mark Dooley

burns & oates

Published by Burns & Oates
A Continuum imprint

The Tower Building   80 Maiden Lane
11 York Road   Suite 704
London SE1 7NX   New York, NY 10038

www.continuumbooks.com

First published 2011

British Library Cataloguing-in-Publication Data
A catalogue record for this book is available from
the British Library.

ISBN: 978-1-4411-1042-8

Typeset by Newgen Imaging Systems Pvt Ltd, Chennai, India
Printed and bound in India

For Matthew

Contents

Introduction   1

1 The Flame of Faith   11

2 What Do We Believe?   28

3 Getting Back to Basics   41

4 From Boredom to Beauty   56

5 What It Means To Be a Priest   73

6 What It Means To Be a Parishioner   93

7 Solace in the Sacraments   105

Conclusion   116

Introduction

I write this book at a time when the Catholic Church is facing its worst crisis since the Reformation. Thanks to the horrifying revelations regarding clerical child sex abuse across the Catholic world, confidence in the Church is at an all-time low. Bishops are resigning, the Pope is under siege and a spirit of fear has possessed the faithful. It seems that the world's oldest institution, one which has, debatably, contributed more to civilization that any other, and one which has cared for and educated millions, has squandered much of its credibility. Many critics claim it has done so, not merely because of the heinous activities of some wicked clerics, but also because it has lost sight of the Gospel message of Jesus Christ. The Church, they argue, is now more an autocratic monarchy than a humble community founded on faith, hope and love. And at its head is the figure of Joseph Ratzinger, a man that writer Christopher Hitchens has labelled an 'elderly villain', and someone who was, at least according to the renegade theologian Hans Küng, responsible for engineering a 'worldwide system of covering up cases of sexual crimes committed by clerics'.[1]

There is no doubt that the Church has lost sight of its mission, but not, I contend, for the reasons given by its detractors. Neither do I believe that Pope Benedict XVI should, on the basis of salacious claims by eminent atheists,

---

1   See Christopher Hitchens, "Topic of Cancer" in *Vanity Fair* (September 2010); Hans Küng, "Open Letter to all Catholic Bishops" in *The Irish Times* (16 April 2010).

be forced to abdicate. Sadly, however, such people are not the only figures calling for the Pope's removal. In a recent edition of the newspaper for which I write, eminent Catholic journalist Peter Stanford, asserted that if the Pope were to abdicate,

> it could potentially send out the most powerful message possible that the Catholic Church acknowledged its past sins and misdemeanours and was determined that they should never happen again. It would say that the Church is an institution committed to the sort of root and branch reform, not just of structures, but of attitudes to sexuality and to the higher calling of the priest that are the fertile soil in which this scandal grew. It would show Benedict as a shepherd and prophet, prepared to make a huge personal sacrifice for the greater good of his Church.[2]

Peter Stanford is no Christopher Hitchens or Richard Dawkins – both of whom are determined to see the pontificate of Pope Benedict XVI implode. Still, he has been around the Catholic world long enough to know that Benedict is arguably the greatest pope of the modern era. That is why, from my perspective, calling for his abdication, especially in the current circumstances, is simply senseless. Stanford is certainly correct when he says that, at 83, Benedict should be enjoying a less pressurized existence. But Joseph Ratzinger has never placed his own interests before that of the Church. And now, in the hour of its gravest trial, he could never countenance abandoning it just because the strain of old age is beginning to show.

---

2   Peter Stanford, 'Saturday Essay' in *Irish Daily Mail* (26 April 2010).

Let me say at the outset why I support the view that Ratzinger was not only the right choice for pope, but an exceptional selection. I do so because much of what I shall subsequently argue in this work is predicated on his vision for the Church. First, despite his years, the Cardinal-electors had enough sense to recognize that no one within their ranks could theologically or intellectually compete with Benedict. Even though he was marginalized by those who surrounded Pope John Paul II, those who entered the papal conclave in 2005 knew that the future pope was somehow set apart. He was by far the best published; his knowledge of the Liturgy was unrivalled, and his insight into the workings of the Church was beyond compare. More than that, however, his writings displayed an inspired understanding of the Eternal. Even his detractors are forced to admit that his three papal encyclicals on faith, hope and charity are works of theological genius and uncommon compassion. It is true, doctrinally speaking, that Pope Benedict is a traditionalist. He believes that the Eucharist should be celebrated with solemnity and in beauty, which is why he lifted restrictions on the Tridentine Mass in 2007. Through its simplicity and magnificence, that old rite has not only enhanced Catholic worship. It has, as witnessed wherever it is celebrated, drawn many people back to daily Mass.

That is all very well, but what of his role in the current abuse crisis? Stanford says it is hard to argue with one Irish mother who, after the Pope recently met with abuse victims in Malta, said: 'Fine for him to cry in Malta, but why wasn't he weeping years ago when he first heard what had been going on? Then we might be further down the line in putting things right than we are.' That is not how the Maltese victims see things. One of those who met the Pope, Joseph Magro, had this to say to one Italian newspaper: 'I did not have any faith in priests. Now, after this moving experience,

I have hope again. You people in Italy have a saint. Do you realise that? You have a saint!'

The truth is that, despite all attempts to associate the Pope with the clerical culture of abuse, he is the one person who has consistently fought what he calls 'this filth'. When in 2001, as Prefect of the Congregation for the Doctrine of the Faith (CDF), he ordered that all files on abuse be sent to his office, it was because he saw how incompetently the cases were being handled by local bishops. There followed, for the first time in church history, a systematic and thorough-going cleansing of the clerical ranks. Hence to accuse Benedict XVI of engineering a 'worldwide system of covering up sexual crimes committed by clerics', is not only false but, in the words of Catholic commentator George Weigel, 'a calumny that I pray was informed in part by ignorance (if culpable ignorance)'.[3] And that is so because, as anyone who has carefully studied Ratzinger's record will know, he was tirelessly working for victims even when his enemies in the Curia were determined to have him sidelined.[4]

Peter Stanford ends his article by asking: 'Would a younger man, young enough to be untouched by the decades of cover-up, do a better job?' He answers: 'Undoubtedly'. But who exactly does he have in mind? All the men – young and old – who made Joseph Ratzinger pope, are acutely aware that no one but he has the requisite wisdom or experience to deal with this terrible controversy. For behind all

---

3   George Weigel, "An Open Letter to Hans Küng" in *First Things* (21 April 2010).

4   For a comprehensive account of Pope Benedict XVI's role in dealing with the abuse crisis, see the stunning volume by Gregory Erlandson and Matthew Bunson, *Pope Benedict XVI and The Sexual Abuse Crisis: Working for Reform and Renewal* (Huntington: Our Sunday Visitor Publishing, 2010).

the misleading headlines and unforgivable attacks on his character, Pope Benedict XVI is a gentle and conscientious pastor who will, if permitted, morally renew the Catholic Church. Above all, however, he is nothing less than a Doctor of the Church – who, in the words of Princeton University Renaissance scholar Anthony Grafton, is 'probably the greatest scholar to rule the Church since [Pope] Innocent III', in the thirteenth century.

I follow Weigel in believing that what most disturbs his detractors is not the putative part the Pope played in concealing clerical sexual crimes, but rather his doctrinal orthodoxy. Few people have sought to rekindle the traditional spirit of the liturgy as enthusiastically as Joseph Ratzinger. As he wrote in 1975:

> One thing is clear: however much the liturgy is simplified and rendered comprehensible, the mystery of God's action operating through the Church's acts must remain untouched. This applies also to the heart of the liturgy: as far as both priest and people are concerned, it is something given, that cannot be manipulated. It partakes of the reality of the whole Church.

He adds: 'We must be far more resolute than heretofore in opposing rationalistic relativism, confusing claptrap and pastoral infantilism. These things degrade the liturgy to the level of a parish tea party and the intelligibility of the popular newspaper.'[5]

This explains why, since his elevation to the see of Peter in 2005, Benedict XVI has prioritized renewal of the liturgy

---

5   Cited in, *The Ratzinger Report: An Exclusive Interview on the State of the Church* (San Francisco: Ignatius Press, 1985), pp. 120–1.

in his programme of Church reform. Contrary to those who argue that his liturgical innovations (such as the return of traditional papal vestments, encouraging the reception of Holy Communion on the tongue and the use of Latin) are illustrations of the Pope's monarchical instincts, I argue that they are essential for revitalizing Catholicism. That is why Joseph Ratzinger is one of the heroes of this short book, and also why his vision for the Church is, I believe, needed now more than ever before. Following Benedict, I contend that the Church will only survive in the modern world if it is confident in its identity. This means rediscovering those traditions which animate the soul of Catholicism, and which are daily manifest in the Holy Mass. As I repeatedly suggest, the Mass lies at the heart of Catholicism, for it is there, in those sacred moments, that Christ reveals Himself to man in time. When that is disregarded or disbelieved, it is then that Catholicism loses its true vocation, which is to make Christ present to all believers in the Eucharist.

Everything else in Catholicism is secondary to the Mass. Hence, if it not celebrated in sacredness, or if it is used to peddle a political agenda, or indeed if it is emptied of its aesthetic splendour, then it risks becoming a source of apathy and boredom. Stated otherwise, when the sacred liturgy is no longer perceived as a miracle due to 'rationalistic relativism, confusing claptrap and pastoral infantilism', Catholics are bound to question the basis of their beliefs. For it is a simple fact that the only connection that most ordinary Catholics have to their church, is through their participation in the Holy Mass. Consequently, if the Eucharist has been reduced to something resembling a 'parish tea party', then it follows that their faith will be tested. Conversely, if the Mass bears witness to the eternal reality of Christ's presence here on earth, it cannot fail to captivate and enthral, notwithstanding the crises which have period-ically engulfed the Church.

My underlying thesis is, therefore, that Pope Benedict is correct in suggesting that rediscovering the beauty of the sacred liturgy is essential for understanding what it means to be a Catholic. This should not, of course, detract from the terrible crimes committed by members of the clergy. But it should serve to remind people of what it is that has sustained Catholicism throughout its 2,000-year history. It should serve to remind them that beyond all the crises and scandals, there are timeless truths which are revealed every day in and through the Mass. And if those truths have been obscured, it is because the liturgy has been subject to a 'spirit of creativity' unleashed in the wake of Vatican II.

As I make clear, this book does not call for a reversal of Vatican II reforms. What it does suggest, however, is that many of the liturgical innovations instituted by Vatican II, were taken in a direction never intended by the Council Fathers. Any careful scrutiny of the original Council docu-ments will reveal that, in the words of Pope Benedict's Master of Liturgical Ceremonies Guido Marini,

> the liturgy does not exist subject to the sporadic modi-fications and arbitrary inventions of one individual or group. The liturgy is not a closed circle in which we decide to meet, perhaps to encourage one another, to feel we are the protagonists of some feast. The liturgy is God's summons to His people to be in His presence; it is the advent of God among us; it is God encountering us in this world.

Acknowledging that is an essential step on the road to Catholic renewal. That is why I devote much of this text to

an examination of why beauty must always be a fundamental feature of Catholic liturgy. In so doing, I rely on
my other great intellectual hero, the English philosopher
Roger Scruton.[6] For it was Scruton, that great thinker of the
beautiful and sublime, who taught me that we belong to a
'sphere of consecrated things', and that beauty is the mark
of that transcendental sphere in time. Without beauty, we
cannot be raised to God, and if our eyes have shifted from
the sacred it is because ugliness has usurped the place once
occupied by its opposite. This is what Scruton terms 'desecration', which is a 'sort of defence against the sacred, an
attempt to destroy its claims'. Our lives, he tells us, 'will be
judged before sacred things; and in order to escape that
judgement, we destroy the thing which seems to accuse us.
And since beauty reminds us of the sacred – and is even a
special form of it – beauty must also be desecrated'.

This 'culture of desecration' has, I contend, swept across
the catholic world with devastating consequences. By taking
possession of priests, parishioners and those responsible for
church music and architecture, it has driven the sacred from
the sanctuaries where it once had its home. This, in turn,
has caused Catholic communities to focus exclusively upon
themselves instead of gazing in awe at Christ. My principal
purpose in this work is to say that unless Catholicism can
once more become Christ-focused, unless it can rediscover
the true beauty and solemnity which once characterized
the celebration of the Mass, it will remain mired in crisis.
For it is only when people and their priests are conformed
to Christ through the power of the sacraments, that the

---

6   The intellectual debt I owe to Scruton is acknowledged in my
    two recent books, *Roger Scruton: The Philosopher on Dover Beach*
    (London: Continuum, 2009), and *The Roger Scruton Reader*
    (London: Continuum, 2009)

consolations of Catholicism will once more be theirs. It is only when they focus on that moment each Sunday, when Christ is made present on the altar of every church, that the point of being a Catholic will become abundantly apparent. If, in other words, the Church is in the midst of a terrible predicament, it is in large part because everything that once kept Catholics focused on Christ has been repudiated in favour of liturgical 'innovation'. This, to repeat, is not to say that the liturgy cannot be adapted to the age. But it does mean that when it comes to timeless things, we ought to tread carefully lest we lose sight of the sacred.

I am aware that what I say in this book will strike many readers as counter-cultural. My response to this is that such people are absolutely correct. For if Catholicism is anything, it is a counter-cultural force which serves to remind us that human life is set apart from the rest of creation. Its message, therefore, is not something which should be subject to change, but one that should be perpetually promulgated in spite of progress. That is why it matters what a Catholic priest wears, how he celebrates the Eucharist, and that he aspire to saintliness. It matters that liturgical norms have a constant character, and that they bear rich witness to the great sacrifice of Calvary and the wonder of the vacant tomb. It also matters that parishioners recognize that when they go to church, it is not simply to gather and pray. Much more than that, it is to witness the miracle of bread and wine being transformed into the Body and Blood of their Redeemer. These are truths which remain untouched by the actions of particular popes, bishops or deviant clergy. And if they are casually brushed aside, it is not surprising that the result is crisis and confusion.

In sum, this book does not aim to provide a new vision for the Church. Neither does it contain some golden for- mula which will enable it to emerge unscathed from its current troubles. What it does offer, however, are some simple suggestions as to how Catholics, clergy and laity alike, might rediscover the riches of their faith. In so doing, my earnest hope is that it will stimulate some much needed reflection regarding the role and function of the Church in a world which has lost its moral compass.

* * *

The idea for this work originated in a series of articles which I published on Catholicism and the abuse crisis in the *Irish Daily Mail*. I am sincerely grateful to all my editors at the *Mail* for their unfailing encouragement and support over many years. I am also very grateful to the many clergy, both in Ireland and across the world, who have urged me to gather my thoughts on Catholicism into a book. I hope that what I have written here will offer them consolation in challenging times. In a very special way, I should like to thank my publisher at Continuum, Robin Baird-Smith, for his friendship and forbearance. Lastly, my greatest debt goes to my wife Laura, and to my dear children David and Matthew.

1

The Flame of Faith

Why be a Catholic? Why, in an age when the Church is submerged in what Pope Paul VI called 'the smoke of Satan', is there still a deep craving for its consolations? How, in the wake of so many heartbreaking revelations concerning child sex abuse, can we Catholics continue to worship in our chapels, kneel before our shrines and receive Christ from those belonging to a tainted clerical caste? Such questions provide of no easy answer, and profoundly preoccupy most, if not all practicing Catholics. Still, those of us who remain loyal to the Church in these troubled times, have no option but to ask why we do so. When faced with such horrors, unquestioning commitment is no longer an option. We need to look deep into the very heart of what it is that, despite the terrible scandals, continues to call on us to sacrifice, surrender and love. Only then will the promised peace of authentic Catholicism be ours.

No Catholic can remain stoic in the face of clerical child abuse. No Catholic can or should make excuses for people who betrayed their vows by committing heinous acts of violence against the innocent, the vulnerable and the pure of heart. And that is because, to be a Catholic, means to belong to one universal body – the Body of Christ. As the whole body suffers when one of its parts is in pain, so all Catholics will suffer when any member of the Church is troubled, abused or violated. If we don't feel the torment of the abused, then we are somehow disconnected from the bloodstream of the body. Just as we ought to suffer the agony of Christ on the Cross, so we must suffer when crucifixion comes to those who least deserve it.

What is most shocking about clerical child abuse for a Catholic is that it is perpetrated by hands that have been ordained to transform the fruit of the vine into the blood of Christ. It is perpetrated by people of prayer and penitence – people who, in the case of clerics, are charged with granting absolution to the faithful. So when it emerges that a priest has lived a double life as pastor and paedophile, the world of the Catholic collapses. In those dire circumstances, you must ponder the awful reality that the hands that gave you Christ on Sunday were those that defiled the dignity of a child on Monday. You have to confront the terrible truth that the person to whom you confessed your sins, thought nothing of committing unforgivable evil. Contemplating that shocking spectre is akin to experiencing a tragic death.

I say that because the effect on a Catholic of such revelations is so profound and fundamental that it can only be compared to the loss of a loved one. It shatters your trust and destroys your hope. It robs you of all certainty and leaves a gaping wound at the centre of your existence. And then you are left with the question: how could people that devoted their lives to the Good Shepherd violate His sheep? Did they not read that powerful passage from sacred scripture: 'Whosoever humbles himself and becomes like this child will be the greatest in the Kingdom of Heaven, and whoever receives one such child in my name receives me. But if anyone causes the downfall of one of these little ones who believe in me, it would be better for him to have a millstone hung around his neck and be drowned in the depths of the sea'?

Time and again throughout the Gospel, Jesus praises and honours children. Time and again, he warns His disciples what would become of them if they inflicted harm 'on these little ones'. For 'I tell you,' He declared, 'they have their angels in heaven, who look continually on the face of my heavenly Father'. And yet not even the voice of the Christ was strong enough to stop the hand of those who, even as they wore the Cross, set about neglecting, torturing and chastising the little souls placed in their care. How, we must ask, could they in all good conscience consecrate the Bread of Life while simultaneously crucifying these little ones? How could they turn the institutions of the Church into chambers of horror? How could they render their sacred vow to Christ so meaningless, so empty, so dead?

As an Irishman, I have seen firsthand the damage done to the Church by corrupt clergy whose actions were not only a betrayal of Christ, but a form of repeated crucifixion. The devastating reports of rape, brutality and heartless cruelty visited upon the innocent by those supposedly acting *in persona Christi*, rendered the Irish speechless. We simply could not comprehend the gravity of the crimes committed by people in the service of an institution with an unrivalled role in Irish society. Through our tears we read the awful accounts of evil, and listened to the terrifying tales of what happened to children in the so-called 'care' of the Irish clergy. One such priest was my old school chaplain, a man whose heinous activities merited a full chapter of the notorious Murphy Report[1] into clerical child sex abuse in the Dublin Archdiocese. Pope Benedict XVI responded for many when, in his Pastoral Letter to the People of Ireland of March 2010, he declared that abusive clergy 'betrayed the

---

1   The Murphy Report is available at www.justice.ie.

trust that was placed in you by innocent young people and their parents, and you must answer for it before Almighty God and before properly constituted tribunals. You have forfeited the esteem of the people of Ireland and brought shame and dishonour upon your confreres'.[2]

And yet, even in the midst of such horror, the flame of faith still flickers. Notwithstanding all the shock and revulsion, Church pews still pulse with ordinary people in search of sanctity. In the course of writing this book, I visited countless parishes in order to assess the damage done to Church attendance in the wake of the revelations. To my surprise, there was no dramatic decline in people attending Sunday Mass. This is not to say, of course, that parishioners are not angry and frustrated. Many of them are hanging on by a thread, while many more are just waiting for the next batch of revelations before breaking loose. In the meantime, they continue to come to Church, emptied of their confidence in the clergy, but still armed with their love of Christ. Among such people are of course the older generation, who clutch their rosaries as if clinging to a heavenly lifeline. More than most, they have been devastated by the abuse scandals. In the twinkling of an eye, the lifelong trust they placed in their priests was reduced to ash. But still they come, shuffling from statue to station, and mumbling those sacred psalms of thanksgiving which drop so effortlessly from their lips. The Church is their constant companion, and its precious comfort is not something they could ever willingly surrender. For them, it is a simple fact of experience that evil is everywhere. It is no surprise, therefore, that it should be found at the very heart of that place where its

---

2   The Pastoral Letter of His Holiness Benedict XVI to the Catholics of Ireland (19 March 2010) is available at www.vatican.va.

opposite resides, and through which eternity stakes its claim on time.

There is, however, something more to it than that. The elderly have been around long enough to know that faith in its purest form is not an optional extra, but a fundamental feature of the human condition. It is not something that you can simply abandon without losing an essential part of yourself. And that is because possessing true faith involves commitment to certain basic tenets which remain unaffected by the actions of mortals. To believe, in other words, is an existential engagement which cannot be expunged when the going gets rough. It is a disposition which directs the very being of the person, and which finds cultivation in those institutional contexts where we, so it is believed, make contact with infinity.

Let me express this in another way: experience allows one to see that society is not, as many in the modern world maintain, an experiment. The view that there is no such thing as human nature is the core belief of what we have come to know as 'postmodernism'. But age and experience are usually enough to convince people of the inherent folly of such ideas. For to endlessly experiment with the self and society, is to squander the political, social and moral wisdom which has been handed down by 'absent genera-tions'. It is to turn one's back on the bequest of the dead for the sake of the present age. It is to assume that society is capable of starting over, of returning to 'Year 0' where the unspoilt innocence of Eden might once more be ours. To many such a view might seem puerile, and they would of course be correct. Still, it has animated the radical sentiments of the French revolutionaries, the Nazis, the Communists and the diabolical regimes of those such as Pol Pot. At some level, all of those people believed that the old traditions of ordinary people are 'inauthentic', and must therefore be erased. It is necessary, they declare, to begin again so as to put things right.

As the French Revolution so dramatically proved, what we sacrifice through such experiments is not just human life, but the social knowledge upon which successful society depends. This was the great message of Edmund Burke's *Reflections on the Revolution in France*. Of course, despite his sympathies for the old religion, Burke was no Catholic. But his great book was, if nothing else, a defence of those quintessentially 'Catholic' traditions which were being tossed, along with countless heads, into buckets at the base of the guillotine. For him, the Church is not simply an institution like any other, but the 'first of our prejudices'. By 'prejudice', Burke did not mean narrow-minded bigotry, but that stock of wisdom which is handed down in the form of norms, customs, rites and rituals. Being the first of our prejudices, the Church preserves the 'early received and uniformly sense of mankind' from 'profanation and ruin'. It fills our hope 'full of immortality' so that we should neither 'look to the paltry pelf of the moment, nor to the temporary and transient praise of the vulgar, but to a solid, permanent existence, in the permanent part of [our] nature'.[3]

The Church stands, in other words, as a monument to our enduring nature as beings in search of more than transient pleasure. It testifies to our indomitable longing for permanence, continuity and social stability. And it does so by being a repository of that ancient wisdom which teaches that ours is not, as Burke writes, a 'partnership in things subservient only to the gross animal existence

---

3   Edmund Burke, *Reflections on the Revolution in France* (New Haven: Yale University Press, 2003), pp. 78–9.

of a temporary and perishable nature'. Rather, it is a partnership in virtue and perfection – one between the living,
the dead and those who have yet to be born. Such is what
Burke majestically calls 'the great primeval contract of
eternal society, linking the higher and lower natures,
connecting the visible and invisible world, according to
a fixed compact sanctioned by the inviolable oath which
holds all physical and moral natures, each in their appointed
place'.[4]

Alone in the modern world, the Catholic Church reso-
lutely upholds that great primeval contract of eternal
society. The older generation of Catholics understand this,
which is why, for them, the flame of faith still flickers. Many
of them witnessed the horrors of the twentieth century, a
period in which human beings were reduced to 'the gross
animal existence of a temporary and perishable nature'.
They know exactly what happens when the sacrifices of the
dead are plundered in the name of 'progress', which is why
they look to their church as that point of intersection
between the living, the deceased and the unborn. This does
not mean that the Catholic Church is anti-modernist, but
only that it seeks to defend the constants of human nature
from baseless experimentation. And it does so by providing
an institutional space where the departed can freely dwell
among their descendants, and where the unborn are forever
factored into the considerations of the living. The Church,
we might say, is a memorial not only to the Victim of
Calvary and all those martyrs who followed Him, but to
every soul who once laid claim to this earth. Or, as the
English philosopher Roger Scruton might put it, Catholicism reminds us that we came from *somewhere* rather than

---

4   Ibid., p. 82.

nowhere, that we are but one phase in an ongoing dialectic between the generations.[5]

Despite all the scandal, torment and suffering visited upon the Church by certain elements within the clergy, this truth remains intact, as indeed it has done throughout all the momentous crises of Catholicism. So too do the basic theological tenets of the faith, which cannot be corrupted by the singularly evil actions of particular people. This, of course, does not mean that the Church need not answer for the crimes of its members. But those crimes do absolutely nothing to alter the foundations of a religion rooted in the soil of Calvary, and one whose bequest to the world is that of faith, hope and love.

Those of us who cling to the consolations of Catholicism, do so, in other words, because the Church connects us to something more than ourselves. Its sacred liturgy enables believers to hear the call of 'ancestral voices'. In so doing, we are reminded that we are dependent creatures, who are here only because of the sacrifices of our dearly departed. We are reminded that ours is but a temporary trusteeship of their moral and spiritual legacy, and that everything we humans do can have a sacred and sacramental character. This means that we can look at the world with merely human eyes, or we can observe it with the eyes of faith. The eyes of faith are those which never lose sight of the transcendent dimension of human existence. They look at the world as if perpetually staring through stained glass windows. Where the scientist sees only sinew and bone, the faithful always see something more – something beyond mere scientific explanation. And that 'something more' is

---

5   See Roger Scruton, *News From Somewhere: On Settling* (London: Continuum, 2004).

not illusory, but is perfectly evident in our capacity to surpass immediacy in the direction of immortality.

No other creature can long for the immortal, but we can. No other creature can stand back from their existence and contemplate not being in the world, but we can. No other creature can sanctify the hours, mourn their dead and purposely make sacrifices for the unborn. But we can, and we do. And the consolation which we receive from doing these things is not a false comfort, but one which enables us to flourish in spite of temporal contingency. Catholicism provides the context in which we can stand between worlds, as it were. It teaches us that the sacramental outlook is not something which we can dispense with and still flourish. Rather, it is the outlook we humans must cultivate if we are to reach our full potential. For that is our particular predicament: we are, by our very nature, suspended between past and future. And everything that we do and think is pervaded by a consciousness of timelessness which will one day become a reality for all. Of course, we can live purely in the moment, driving away all thoughts of death and transcendence. But is that a life worth living? Can it cope with the guilt and regret which will inevitably stake their claim on those who would deny them, and can it endure the alienation and frustration that result from letting one's true human potential rest unfulfilled?

In the sacred space which Catholicism opens up, a space which seeks to satisfy our transcendent longings, the alienation of the present age is surmounted. For what it offers is, in effect, nothing less than a revelation of the Divine here on earth. Through the sacraments, we are not only made conscious of our place in the eternal society, but we are given a glimpse into its very heart. The dead *literally* become present to the living, while summoning us to live lives worthy of their sacrifice. In this sacramental space, we are not invited to look through, or beyond the objects which it contains in order to experience eternity. If anything, eternity emerges *in the midst* of these objects. The sacred Host is, the Catholic believes, a revelation of Christ Himself. Christ is, however, not simply hiding behind the Host, but is there *fully present* in its fabric. That is why, as we shall see, the shape and structure of a Catholic church is not something which can be sacrificed to contemporary architectural fads. It must reflect the fact that Christ Himself, along with all the dead, is there among the living. This is not a manifestation of the ordinary or the purely natural, but of the extra-ordinary and the supernatural. That being so, shouldn't the space in which it emerges be no less startling or extraordinary than the events themselves?

Catholicism presents an antidote to the agony of knowing, to paraphrase Scruton, that we are 'in the world, yet not entirely of it'. Not only does it offer salvation from our fallen state which is manifest in selfishness and sin, but through its ancient rites and rituals we are transported to the very precipice of time. We are brought to a place on the periphery of mortal existence, and across whose horizon we can glimpse our eternal home. This means that if Catholicism is about anything it is about *homecoming*. It is about reconciliation and atonement, communion and confession. It is about all those things which overcome division and rupture, and which enable a person to be 'at-one' with himself and his Creator. It is a religion through which hopes can be made real, aspirations actualized, and sorrows salved. Most of all, it is about learning how to discover, in the midst of the world, a presentiment of paradise.

All of this is made possible by the fact that the Catholic Church is more than just an institution. In essence, it resembles a person, in as much as we can relate to it, belong to it, weep for it, suffer with it, and die in its arms. The Church is not a static structure, but is forever evolving in accordance with experience. Hers is a living tradition which beats in sync with the heart of each of its members. And, like every mother, she provides a home to which all wayward pilgrims can return in peace at journey's end. By this I mean that she is a living link, not only to the dead and the unborn, but to the very foundations of the faith. Through her you can, like the prodigal son, return to the ultimate source, and savour the joy which it alone can supply.

I know this because I was once that prodigal son. My youth was characterized by strong Christian devotion. That was a time when my country was predominantly Catholic, and when priests had a status in society which far outranked most other professions. Like so many of my generation, I served Mass, could recite the Catechism, entertained the possibility of becoming a priest and was genuinely committed to my religious obligations. And so it was until the first major cracks in the old edifice began to emerge. In 1992, it was reported that the Bishop of Galway, Dr Eamon Casey, had fathered a child and had gone to some lengths to keep the matter secret. I was then completing an undergraduate degree in philosophy at University College Dublin (UCD), and was preparing to undertake a Masters degree in the same subject. As the revelations about Bishop Casey unfolded, followed by the first disclosures regarding clerical child sex abuse, I became intoxicated by currents in contemporary philosophy. Nietzsche's proclamation that 'God is Dead', Jean Paul Sartre's claim that 'Man is what he makes of himself', and Michel Foucault's contention that truth is not a reflection of reality, but something in the service of power, all began to ring true. And when I was appointed to my first job as lecturer in philosophy at UCD in 1993, it was this soulless stuff which became my stock in trade.

Still, something deep within me rejected the person I had become. Throughout my years in this intellectual wilderness, I never quite believed in what I was teaching or writing. My students loved it, of course, as it gave intellectual justification to their repudiation of authority. For that is what all such currents of thought are: an attempt to undermine all those inherited things which have traditionally commanded obedience. Hence the 'Truth' is sacrificed in favour of multiple interpretations. God, the ultimate authority, is dethroned and replaced by a void at the heart of creation. Even Jesus, at least as He appears in the gospels, is rejected as being too symbolic of an authoritarian church intent on wielding power instead of identifying with the downtrodden. This is Jesus, the 'radical egalitarian' who, were He to return, would condemn the Roman Catholic Church as being excessively hierarchical and elitist.[6]

For years, I found myself attending conferences, writing books and articles that championed this theology of liberation. I frequented circles in which the 'death of God' slogan was bandied about by people who should have known better. I even had the dubious honour of sharing an evening with the renegade theologian Fr Hans Küng, who passed those hours complaining how Pope John Paul II and Cardinal Ratzinger had consistently ignored his call for a private audience. During such moments, it became patently clear to me that, somewhere along the line, I had taken a wrong turn. I had sold out to something which rejected everything that I knew, deep down, rendered human life worthwhile. In so doing, I had come to know a lot about the historical Jesus, but had lost touch with the Jesus of

---

6   See, for example, John Dominic Crossan, *Jesus: A Revolutionary Biography* (San Francisco: HarperCollins, 1995).

faith – that figure who raised the dead, cured the sick and fed the hungry. I had wandered far from home in the direction of nothingness and nowhere. I had abandoned comfort and consolation for alienation and estrangement, to the point where I could no longer hear those sweet and saving words: 'Come to Me, all you who are weary and burdened, and I will give you rest. Take my yoke and learn from Me, for I am gentle and humble in heart, and you will find rest for your souls.'

I was lost. Still, I knew there was a path somewhere to take me home and I stumbled upon it quite unexpectedly. Shortly after being appointed John Henry Newman Scholar in Theology at UCD in 1998, a former student requested to meet with me. She told me that, in teaching her the counsel of despair as proclaimed by the likes of Nietzsche, I had destroyed her faith. She acknowledged that I had not done so purposely, but that my passion for this theology of alienation had profoundly affected her life. I mumbled that, as a philosopher, it was my job to get students to question their prejudices. But then I stopped short, for I knew that I was attempting to defend the indefensible. I knew that I had seriously undermined the most sacred thing that this young person possessed – her belief in a transcendent and loving Creator who offered her the joy and peace which surpasses all comprehension. I had, however inadvertently, robbed her of something which atheists routinely scoff at, but which believers know is the only sure path to lasting satisfaction.

And then, that young woman who, while studying under my tutelage, looked tired and drawn, but who now appeared truly radiant, reached out and said: 'It is OK. I have since rediscovered my faith and have put the past behind me. I have come home and all is well.' Even though the Church was then in deep crisis, that brave young soul had the courage to look beyond the sordid behaviour of some of its members. For her, the Catholic Church could not be judged solely on the sinful deeds of a minority of its present trustees. For to do so, would be to ignore the fact that the primary purpose of the Church is to bring believers face to face with Jesus Christ in the Holy Eucharist. That is why Catholicism cannot be reduced to the sum of its present guardians. It is, to repeat, that which sustains the 'eternal society' through time, having witnessed first-hand the miraculous events from which it was born. By linking us to the dead through the Resurrection, we have in the Church a way of transcending temporal alienation. We have, through her, a means of reclaiming our origins – of returning, as it were, to that place whence we came. If the world gives only isolation and rupture, the Church provides continuity through communion with Christ. It was this beautiful reality which I had sullied for my student, but which she, in trust and faith, had reclaimed as her rightful bequest. She had, in other words, stopped learning from me. Now, she was learning from Him, and had found rest for her soul.

My encounter with that young woman had a profound impact on my life. For one thing, I knew that I could no longer travel with the atheists. I knew that for many years I had been living a lie, one which had advanced my career, but which had caused me immense personal pain in the process. My former student radiated happiness in abundance. I, on the other hand, was permanently miserable. It was then I realized that I had become a typical product of the liberal urge to stand alone in defiance of my kind. My intellectual pursuits had convinced me that the beliefs of ordinary people were unfounded and thus worthy of condemnation. But my student persuaded me that I was wrong – very wrong to have followed a road which, by castigating simplicity, leads only to cynicism. In that moment,

I knew for the very first time what Jesus meant when he declared: 'I tell you the truth, unless you change and become like little children, you will never enter the kingdom of heaven.' In saying this, Christ was not demanding childishness, but simplicity. Simplicity of this kind is not anti-intellectual or irrational, but is a way of living one's life that respects the humble customs and social conventions which characterize everyday existence. It is a disposition which acknowledges that before the 'I' there is a 'We' – a web of personal, social and moral obligations which I did not form, but which formed and shaped me into the person that I am. This does not mean, of course, that I should uncritically accept that which is handed down to me. But it does mean that when criticism is called for, it ought to be undertaken in a sensitive spirit, especially when dealing with matters of faith.

Shortly after that fateful meeting with my ex-student, I was drawn back to the Catholic Church. Like the Prodigal Son, I had wandered far from home in a spirit of disobedience. But when, one day, I took my first steps inside an old and musty chapel, I instantly understood why Catholics exude joy, while those who opt for alienation are absorbed by anger. As I approached the altar, I was moved to genuflect before the tabernacle. I had done so a million times in my youth, but now I did so with tears and tenderness. For here was I, a man who had reasoned his way out of the Church, but who now found himself acutely aware of reason's limitations. As I knelt there all alone before those small golden doors, the aroma of altar wine and incense hanging in the air, I realized that I was once again in communion with the eternal society. I had been cut adrift from my origins, but now I was settled in a place which offered the security of home. And in the weeks and months which followed, I was incorporated back into my faith community – a gentle fellowship bound together by a shared love of Christ and His Church. It is a community of those whose hope perforates the fabric of time, people who have chosen 'at-one-ment' over estrangement, communion over separation, and reconciliation over rebellion.

It was then that I began to look once more upon the world with the eyes of faith. In so doing, I could see exquisite colour where once I noticed only grey. My surroundings began to assume a sacramental character: things which I previously claimed by right, I now perceived as gifts of divine grace. No longer was I conscious of what Miguel de Unamuno termed 'the tragic sense of life'. For me, life had suddenly become a joy, one in which the nihilism of Sartre and Nietzsche rang hollow. Through the Church, I had rediscovered an avenue which led me right back to that day of redemption, a day when His blood was spilled for me and for all men so that transgressions might be forgiven. Indeed, everywhere I looked I began to perceive the glow of paradise. Sartre famously declared that 'Hell is other people'. But to me, other people were now a source of love and light, conveying, as they do, a sense of the sacred here on earth.

In the end, the flame of faith still flickers because the life of Catholics is infused with that love and light. For them, faith is not some irrational leap in the dark. Neither is it something which denies the facts of science. It is, if anything, a search for meaning and value in the midst of the material world. Faith teaches us, in other words, that there is more to life than is dreamt of in Darwin's theories. When, for example, we encounter love and longing, we have a revelation of something which exceeds natural explanation. When we reason morally, we do so, not in the service of our genes, but in opposition to our basic instincts. Faith is a revelation of this reality – the reality that our world has, to repeat, a sacramental quality. And it is the Church, through its beautiful rituals and timeless traditions, which constantly reminds the faithful of that fact. That is why Catholicism continues to endure through its countless crises, and why it remains a source of solace for so many. And it is why I am so grateful to be a Catholic, and why I shall never again be tempted to search for the living in the place of the dead.

2

What Do We Believe?

Still, let no one doubt that Catholicism is suffering. Let no one deny that while the Church is thriving throughout much of the Southern Hemisphere, it faces serious challenges in Europe, the United States and elsewhere in the developed world. The horror of the sex abuse scandals has left even the most faithful feeling betrayed, shocked and deeply wounded. Meanwhile, the Catholic hierarchy in those countries most affected, has responded inadequately and, at times, insensitively. In Ireland, for example, the bishops reacted to the litany of horrors either by publicly squabbling or by remaining silent. The sight of prelates resigning across Europe either because of inaction, or because of their complicity in clerical child abuse cases, has tainted the Catholic faith beyond recognition. How, many ask, can a church responsible for so much agony survive?

In what follows, I want to propose a programme for Catholic renewal in the wake of this terrible episode in the Church's history. I want to suggest that the portrait of Catholicism, which I painted in the previous chapter, is not merely an ideal but a reality which all Catholics can and must experience if their church is to endure. If the flame of faith still burns, it is only because the true essence of the faith, as revealed in the beauty of the sacraments, is still present at least in some small pockets of the 'Old World'.

Elsewhere, however, the ancient rites and rituals, which enable people to see with the eyes of faith, have been diminished to the point of extinction. In such places, the splendour and majesty of the Catholic liturgy has been supplanted by what Roger Scruton once appropriately labelled, the 'pestilence of pulpit politics'. Writing in *The Times* back in 1983, Scruton condemned The National Conference of Roman Catholic Priests as follows:

> The increasing predominance of conferences in pastoral affairs is part of the process whereby the Roman Catholic Church has been transformed from a prescriptive authority, whose currency is faith, to a debating chamber, dealing in the inflationary coinage of opinion. It is inevitable that such a body should begin to turn away from what matters in religion, the eternal verities, towards what, *sub specie aeternitatis* [under the aspect of eternity], matters least of all – the affairs of this world, which can be the subject of opinion only because they lie outside the domain of faith.[1]

Return to faith, in other words, and the true meaning of Catholicism will once again shine forth. Stop seeking to make Catholicism politically relevant, for that is to lose sight of our real vocation as Catholics. Which is what, exactly? In the words of that extraordinary cleric, Monsignor A. N. Gilbey of Cambridge:

> To make a true contribution to putting the world right, we must first establish the kingdom of God in our own

---

1   Roger Scruton, 'The Pestilence of Pulpit Politics' in *Untimely Tracts* (London: The Macmillan Press, 1987), p. 73.

hearts. This primary duty is ours all the time and any effect we have outside ourselves will be either an overflow, a consequence or an instrument of that. The primary province for each of us is not the Third World but our own hearts. The achievement of sanctity is the complete fulfilment of each man's vocation. It will have repercussions outside ourselves, though it may have absolutely none that the world can see. Consider the life of an enclosed contemplative whose effect on the world is literally immeasurable. We may not see the consequences, but the good a contemplative does is beyond our power to measure . . . Each man's vocation is unique and singular to himself and he achieves sanctity by trying to fulfil it. It is something solely between himself and Almighty God.[2]

At their best, Catholics are not political. This, of course, is not to say that Catholicism should desist from contributing to public or political debate. But if such interventions are at the expense of seeking personal salvation, then they count for nothing. Faith is not, in other words, a matter of trying to change the world, but of trying to change oneself in conformity with the Gospel. It is about practising Christianity, in such a way that you shift your gaze from the troubles of this realm to the peace of the next. For the Catholic, this does not mean taking flight from reality. If anything, it means attuning oneself to its sacramental character by seeing all people, things and events as both a work of grace and a reflection of God's presence in our daily lives.

---

2   Monsignor A. N. Gilbey, *We Believe: A Presentation of the Catholic Faith* (London: Bellew Publishing, 1994), p. 11.

It seems obvious to me that the primary reason for the loss of such 'personal' faith is this 'pestilence of pulpit politics'. Since the Second Vatican Council, there has been a concerted effort across the English-speaking Catholic world to shift focus from the cultivation of faith towards an emphasis on political and social concerns. This has led, quite predictably, to a ransacking of the sacramental ethos of Catholicism, and thus to a neglect of those very features of the Catholic faith which make it potentially so fulfilling. In a subsequent chapter, I will explain why I believe certain elements within the clergy are to blame for much of this neglect, and for the inevitable falloff in belief which it engenders. For now, however, I want to further explore Monsignor Gilbey's claim that our primary duty, as Catholics, is to 'establish the kingdom of God in our own hearts'. And I want to do so because one of the major consequences of this shift away from the sacramental life in recent decades has been a loss of purpose for many Catholics. To put the matter very simply: in a world where the Church seems at times more preoccupied with climate change than with Christ, even the most devout struggle with what it is they are supposed to believe, and how that belief should be expressed. That is why, if the Church is to weather the storm, it must get back to basics by unashamedly proclaiming fundamental Catholic doctrine, and by redirecting its gaze from the 'paltry pelf of the moment' back towards those 'eternal verities' which enable us to glimpse our heavenly home.

So what is it that Catholics are meant to believe? The answer is to be found in that great prayer which we know as The Creed, and which every practising Catholic recites at Mass each Sunday. It is also to be found in condensed form in The Apostles' Creed – a synoptic profession of faith in the Holy Trinity. It begins by declaring belief in the ineffable majesty of 'God, the Father almighty, creator of heaven and earth'. But how are we to treat such a declaration in a world dominated by science, or in a culture which has long since condemned the so-called myth of creation? It seems to me that Catholics should not shirk the challenge of science. If Catholics are to have credibility, they must cease pretending as though dramatic scientific discoveries are not happening, or as though they tell us nothing about the origin of the universe. If anything, we should marvel at the fact that human beings are capable of casting such a radiant light on the source and structure of the cosmos. We should stand in awe at the findings of those who intelligently explain evolution, for there is nothing in either astrophysics or Darwinism which puts paid to the existence of God the creator. The fact that we evolved, in other words, tells us nothing about *why* we evolved. And despite the monumental advances in astrophysics, we are still none the wiser as to the original cause of creation.

I say this notwithstanding the recent claims made by astrophysicist Professor Stephen Hawking in his book *The Grand Design*.[3] Hawking asserts that 'because there is a law such as gravity, the universe can and will create itself from nothing', and 'spontaneous creation is the reason there is something rather than nothing, why the universe exists, why we exist'. Put simply, the laws of physics render God redundant. At its best, religion would not run from Hawking's claims, but would simply point out that it seems illogical to say that something can be created from nothing. To state that because there is a law of gravity, spontaneous creation is the reason why there is something rather than

---

3   Stephen Hawking and Leonard Mlodinow, *The Grand Design* (New York: Bantam Press, 2010).

nothing, begs the obvious question: where did the law of gravity come from? We do not answer that question by saying it came from nowhere, for that only serves to stymie enquiry where more is surely required.

Catholicism looks upon creation as a mystery, not because it has nothing to say, but because it recognizes that questions regarding the ultimate cause cannot be prematurely terminated. There is always one more 'why?' which shatters the illusion of scientific certainty. But there is also the fact that from creation flowed consciousness, something without which the secrets of the universe would remain permanently sealed. What I am suggesting is this: like religion, science is the product of human consciousness. The universe, in other words, makes itself known through us. And so long as we are unable to furnish a complete definition of consciousness, we must remain satisfied that the 'absolute knowledge' which Hawking dreams of is beyond our scope. We might say that religion, in teaching that there is a mystery at the heart of creation, acts as a barrier to man's perennial quest to dethrone God. In so doing, it inoculates against the arrogance of thinking that human limitation is a hindrance.[4]

Richard Dawkins tells us that God is a delusion, and that those who seek His consolation are like infants in search of a pacifier. There is, of course, nothing original in that view. Nietzsche said as much when he proclaimed God's death back in 1882, and when he declared that Christianity is nothing more than a 'slave morality' and the prime cause

---

4   This line of argument is deftly articulated by Scruton in *The Face of God*, the subject of The Gifford Lectures presented at St. Andrew's University in May, 2010. The lectures are due to be published under the same title by Continuum International in 2011. See also Mark Dooley, *Roger Scruton*, chapter 1.

of resentment. Indeed, the history of atheism is littered with such pronouncements, all of them insisting that where believers see something there is in fact nothing. In one of his most arresting passages, Nietzsche hauntingly illustrates the reality of man's condition in a world from which God has fled:

> In some remote corner of the universe, poured out and glittering in innumerable solar systems, there once was star on which clever animals invented knowledge. That was the haughtiest and most mendacious minute of 'world history' – yet only a minute. After nature had drawn a few breaths the star grew cold, and the clever animals had to die.[5]

You and I are those poor 'clever animals' who believe that beyond our world there is another where time and death have no purchase. But we are deluded, according to Nietzsche, for there is no 'higher' purpose in nature or in humanity which can justify our airs and graces. We are for him like all creatures, subject to the whim of contingency and chance. What awaits us is not immortality, but only the grave. No more, no less.

Nietzsche and Dawkins are right: we are specks on a little star, whose 'anonymous rumbling' is but a faint murmur in a universe so vast that it defies human comprehension. But this, once again, does nothing to refute the existence of God as it fails to answer that old philosophical conundrum: Why is there something rather than nothing? For the one who sees with the eyes of faith, scientific rationality does

---

5   Friedrich Nietzsche, 'On Truth and Lie in an Extra-Moral Sense' in Walter Kaufmann (ed.) *The Portable Nietzsche* (New York: Random House, 1980), p. 42.

not act as a barrier. This is not to say that faith is irrational, but simply that it penetrates into places where the eyes of science are blind. A robust faith will, in other words, go the distance with science. But it refuses to stop at the artificial limits imposed upon it by a form of reason, whose parameters are strictly demarcated by science. It is not, for example, irrational to see as plausible the proofs for God's existence as supplied by Sts Anselm or Thomas Aquinas. Neither is it absurd to look for a transcendent meaning where the scientist can furnish only a causal account. Or, as Scruton puts it: 'Our reason over-reaches the bounds of science, and this is not a deficiency in our reason, but a limitation in science.' To profess one's faith in 'God, the Father almighty, creator of heaven and earth' is not, therefore, to succumb to stupidity. If anything, it is an acknowledgement that there are features of this world which serve as intimations of a transcendent reality which science can never hope to explain.

That is what it means to stand in awe before creation, and it is something which Catholicism seeks to cultivate in each of its adherents. If the object of science is to become 'master and possessor of nature', the purpose of Catholicism is to engender humility in the face of what Immanuel Kant called 'the starry heavens above and the moral law within'. Catholic faith stands, that is, on the threshold of scientific knowledge, but refuses to believe that what lies on the other side is mere nothingness. It has the intellectual honesty to recognize that there are things in this world which humanity can never hope to fully fathom, but which can still give meaning and purpose to those who trust in them. For ultimately that is what faith is: an unwavering belief that beyond the furthest frontier there is not mere anonymity, but a loving creator who we deem to call 'Father'. It was such faith which, despite all his tragedy and misfortune, allowed Job to fall on his knees and declare: 'I know that you can do all things and that no purpose is beyond you.' It was such faith which enabled Abraham to take his son Isaac to Mount Moriah as an offering to the Lord. In so doing, he hoped against hope that God, in all His mercy, would not ultimately seize Isaac as a sacrifice. His hope paid off, for Abraham believed that no matter how dire the circumstances 'the Lord will provide'. And it was such sublime trust which fortified Christ as he prayed in agony on the Mount of Olives: 'My Father, if it is possible, let this cup pass me by. Yet not my will but yours.' With these words, Christ testified to the fact that only with the faith of a child can we truly fulfil our Christian mission. If, in other words, we believe that man is a product of nothingness, that he is solely what he makes of himself, then true sacrifice and virtue are worthless. But if we are at least open to the possibility that beyond the starry heavens there is something more than science concedes, then hope springs eternal.

'Blessed are those who have not seen and yet still believe'. Few of us have seen, and yet many believe. We believe not only in the Creator of heaven and earth, but also in Jesus Christ, 'His only Son, our Lord, who was conceived by the power of the Holy Spirit and born of the Virgin Mary'. We believe, in other words, that in order to reconcile time and eternity, the Creator emptied Himself by becoming human. Furthermore, we accept that he did so through a lowly virgin who was, herself, immaculately conceived. And it doesn't stop there: we also believe that, at the age of 30, Jesus began a three-year ministry which involved proclaiming the Kingdom of God, curing the sick and raising people from the dead. Then, after giving mankind the gift of the Holy Eucharist – the means by which God and man could forever commune – 'He suffered under Pontius Pilate, was crucified, died, and was buried. He descended to the dead. On the third day He rose again. He ascended into heaven, and is seated at the right hand of the Father'. That, for Catholics, is not a fancy fable, but the very core of their faith. This does not mean that it is easy to accept or believe. But who said being Catholic is easy?

Faith challenges. It invites us to tiptoe across the barrier separating time and eternity, a journey which demands an abundance of trust. After all, what we are asked to follow is not someone visibly glorified by God. Indeed, as that great theologian of the nineteenth century Søren Kierkegaard put it, the person who claimed to be the Son of God did not speak to us while sitting 'in glory at the Father's right hand. No, 'from glory he has not spoken a word', but only from 'His state of abasement'. Christ is the supreme object of faith, not because of what He did, but because of what He was. The signs and miracles He performed gave witness to His eternal glory, and those who witnessed them believed. But for those who did not experience the miracles or witness the Resurrection, there is only faith. No amount of time or theology can change the fact that when we proclaim ourselves Catholic, we do so not because we can definitively *prove* that Jesus was the Christ, but because we *believe* that He was. We believe, in other words, that this 'lowly, destitute man with twelve poor disciples from the commonest class of people'[6] was God incarnate. That, for Kierkegaard, is an 'offence' to reason. Is this to say that belief in Jesus is irrational? Not in the least. But it is to assert that having faith in Him is, as Scruton suggests, 'to stake a claim in territory where the writ of reason does not run'.

---

6   Søren Kierkegaard, *Practice in Christianity* (New Jersey: Princeton University Press, 1991), p. 37.

Believing in Jesus Christ means proclaiming, despite all the evidence to the contrary, that He *is* the Son of God. It demands *imitating* Him, and seeing His life as the pattern of our existence here on earth. This involves making sacrifices for others a pivotal feature of one's own life. It involves taking that excruciating journey to Calvary in an effort to abandon self in favour of those who need us most. It involves turning the other cheek, forgiving one's enemies and spreading love without measure. It involves following His mother Mary in saying 'Yes' to everything He asks of us, even unto the point of ridicule. But it also involves worship, for none of this would be humanly possible if we were not constantly reminded of *who it is* that we are invited to imitate. If there is a point in being a Catholic, it is that we can become one with the object of our faith. We believe that we can directly commune with the person of Christ through the celebration of the Holy Eucharist, through the sacraments, prayer and what Kierkegaard called 'works of love'. And here, once again, we return to that very Catholic word: *atonement*. Catholics do not wish only to emulate the Christ figure, but to be *at one* with Him. They want, that is, to be fully reconciled with their creator through the saving power of the God-man.

Communion, for Catholics, is the gateway to paradise, which is why the *Catechism of the Catholic Church* calls the Eucharist 'the source and summit of the Christian life'. For at its heart 'is contained the whole spiritual good of the Church, namely Christ Himself . . .' This explains why nothing should matter more to a Catholic than the Holy Mass. It is there while kneeling at the foot of the altar that the eyes of faith see farthest. They see, as Saint John Vianney wrote, 'deep into eternity'. In that moment, when the simple gifts of bread and wine are mysteriously transformed into the Body and Blood of Christ, the sacramental character of human existence is made abundantly evident. In defiance of our senses, we peer through the Host towards the supernatural reality it conceals. And when we ingest it, we do so in the belief that the division between heaven and earth has been bridged by this tiny slice of sacred bread. If the Mass is crucial for a Catholic, it is because true communion with Christ is impossible outside it. Hence, as I shall suggest in subsequent chapters, the way the Mass is celebrated is not something which should be up for grabs. And that is so because, if you truly believe that Christ becomes present at the moment of consecration, then it matters how we prepare for His coming. Get that right, in other words, and everything else will naturally fall into place.

The time that Catholics spend in church informs and impacts on the moments that we don't. That is why we conclude The Apostles' Creed by saying: 'I believe in the Holy Spirit, the Holy Catholic Church, the communion of saints, the forgiveness of sins, the resurrection of the body, and the life everlasting.' Through the Catholic Church, we receive the Holy Spirit in Confirmation. It is there that we learn to emulate and communicate with the saints, whose shrines summon us to that other more sacred sphere. It is there, as discussed in the last chapter, that we are baptized into the great eternal society, where the voices of the dead and the unborn chime harmoniously with those of the living. It is there that the burden of our faults and failings is lifted from our shoulders through the consolation of confession. And it is from that piece of hallowed soil that the spirit of the departed ascends, along with the incense, in the direction of its heavenly home.

If Catholics believe all that, it is because they have before them the example of those who lived their lives suspended between time and eternity. In living a sacramental existence, the saints did not take their eyes off this world so as to focus on something wholly immaterial. The very best of them did what I have been suggesting ordinary Catholics should also do: they looked at the things of this world for signs of the next. This is achieved, first and foremost, by following Monsignor Gilbey and establishing the Kingdom of God in our own hearts. If, in other words, we do not begin by striving to know Christ on a personal level, we will never be sufficiently capable of imitating Him. The sacraments are the portals through which the light of Christ shines. They thus enable us to become one with Him, and, in so doing, to reveal His glory to the rest of creation. The sacramental life should not, therefore, be considered an ascetic existence. If anything, it is a life whose primary purpose is to expose, in one's own person, the beauty that only the eyes of faith can truly see in all its abundance. It is, as such, a life in which beauty and the sublime matter. For how else but in beauty can the Creator of heaven and earth be revealed? How else can the Saviour of mankind – He who perished so that humanity might be redeemed – be made manifest except in splendour?

Finding Christ in the world is, in sum, a matter of looking for Him in the right places. But we cannot do that without first meeting Him in faith. We cannot do it without conforming ourselves to Him through the sacraments, those gifts which enable Catholics to peer into paradise. And if, after doing this, we play a part in changing the world it will simply be an 'overflow' of that vital experience. Hence the reason for being a Catholic is not, in the first instance, to revolutionize or reform the social and political landscape. It is to cultivate true belief in Christ and, in so doing, to become a better human being. Such is the sole route to saintliness, and those of us who refuse to take it remain stranded on that lonely road to nowhere.

3

Getting Back to Basics

All of this amounts to saying that the Catholic Church
contains within itself the memory of its roots and origins,
and that we can tap into that sacred storehouse through
faith in the sacraments. But what if the Church itself is on
the road to nowhere? What if the crisis in Catholicism is a
consequence of the Church's repudiation of its own heritage? How then can Catholics hope to conform themselves
to Christ in the manner I outlined in the last chapter? It
seems to me that one of the central reasons for the current
catastrophe, is that the Church has lost touch with both its
memory and its true mission. By prioritizing pulpit politics
over personal salvation, it has rejected homecoming in
favour of alienation. It has severed its connection with the
great eternal society, opting instead for the paltry pelf of the
moment. It has become a church more invested in time than
in what lies beyond it. It is as if, at some point, it began to
believe that its detractors were correct when they declared
the Church ripe for deconstruction.

I say that because, long before the clerical child sex abuse
scandal came to light, the Catholic Church was already in
difficulty. Long before we knew anything about the true
horror and scale of that scandal, it was obvious that Catholic devotion, especially in Europe, was in decline. There
were, of course, many reasons for this – not least the secular

spirit which took hold in the 1960s. What I want to suggest, however, is that notwithstanding these socio-cultural challenges, the Church, by abandoning her ancient rites and rituals for a dumbed-down and user-friendly liturgy in the period following Vatican II, did much to exacerbate its difficulties. My objective in this chapter is to argue, therefore, that only by getting back to basics will the Church experience real renewal. First, however, I want to take a brief detour through some recent church history as a way of justifying my contention that recent reforms of the sacred liturgy are at the core of the Church's dilemmas.

Like most of those who had previously occupied the See of Peter, the popes of the twentieth century saw their role as guardians of a sacred tradition stretching back to Calvary. From Pope Pius X (1903–1914) to Pope John XXIII (1958–1963), the modern papacy was characterized by adherence to timeless liturgical norms. The beauty of the old vestments, the glorious Gregorian hymns and the Latin language, all bore witness to the fact that the Catholic Church is not fully of this world, and that, in its sacred simplicity, the old liturgy could reveal the true majesty and splendour of eternity. When he summoned the Second Vatican Council in 1962, Pope John XXIII could not have envisaged the deviation from this great tradition that would, at times, result.

This is not to say that Pope John was mistaken in calling Vatican II. All institutions, no matter how venerable or ancient, require reform. But reform does not equal revolution, which seeks only to wipe clean the slate of history. Reform is something altogether more gentle and rational – something which looks upon what we have inherited with gratitude and which understands that such things have survived only because many have sacrificed in their name. There were many who contributed to the Second Vatican

Council in that vein, not least Karol Wojtyla (the future Pope John Paul II) and Joseph Ratzinger (the future Pope Benedict XVI). But there were others who seized upon the opportunity of the Council to deconstruct many of the Church's old habits and customs. Such people were determined to stamp out the legacy of Pope Pius XII (1939–1958), who they believed had suffocated the Church in the post-War period. In so far as the Church today looks nothing like it did upon the death of Pius XII, it can be said that they succeeded. And they did so thanks, in no small part, to the pontificate of Paul VI (1963–1978).

On the surface, Pope Paul was a traditionalist. He had served as a close assistant to Pius XII, and, in the words of Church historian Eamon Duffy, he shared 'something of Pius XII's mystically exalted view of the papacy'.[1] He was also a highly cultivated and sensitive man who loved the church whose shepherd he became. But what Paul VI failed to do was heed the warning he himself issued when John XXIII first called the Council: 'This holy old boy doesn't realise what a hornet's nest he's stirring up.' For if it the case that Pope John shook the nest, then Pope Paul let the hornets lose. And he did so because, by failing to take the temperature of those turbulent times, and by refusing to oversee the implementation of the Council's decrees with sufficient papal authority, he inadvertently inaugurated what Pope Benedict XVI has termed a 'hermeneutics of rupture' within the Church.[2]

---

1   Eamon Duffy, *Saints and Sinners: A History of the Popes* (New Haven and London: Yale University Press, 1997), p. 268.
2   The one exception to this trend was the Pope's resolute refusal to concede on artificial birth control. See Humanae Vitae (5 July 1968), available at www.vatican.va. The fact that Paul VI reigned

Nowhere was this more evident than in the way the liturgy was restructured. Gone were the majestic practices which characterized the old Latin rite, only to be replaced by modernist architecture, sloppy and creative liturgy, contemporary music and kitsch art. The old marble altars were either demolished or 'adapted' to suit the new Mass of Paul VI. The solemn spectacle of priest and congregation facing East in anticipation of the risen Christ, was forgotten in favour of priest turning towards the congregation. To many, it seemed as if the Church was somehow becoming disconnected from its celestial roots. It was as if it sought to embrace the spirit of disobedience which animated so much of the cultural and social life of the 1960s and 1970s. In his heart Pope Paul VI knew this which is why, during the final years of his pontificate, he succumbed to crippling prevarication and inner torment. The Church was in crisis, priests were leaving in their thousands, and the Pope had lost much of his popularity and authority.

With enormous evangelical zeal, Pope John Paul II sought to restore the profile of the papacy in the wake of Paul VI's demise in 1978. His countless foreign trips, his confrontation with Communism and his powerful personality not only restored the institution of the papacy to its rightful position, but arguably made it the most visible institution on earth. In many ways, John Paul was more akin to Pius XII: he was a deeply conservative man possessed of great personal charisma and authority. And like Pius, he was aware that for the papacy to be effective it must command obedience – hence his crackdown on Liberation Theology and his so-called 'silencing' of theologians such as Hans

---

for a further decade after the publication of Humanae Vitae, and yet never wrote another encyclical, tells its own story.

Küng and Leonardo Boff. While this made him deeply
unpopular with liberal forces both within and beyond the
Church – people who regarded him as a divisive and
retrograde figure – it did nothing to dent his universal
attractiveness and enduring appeal.

What Pope John Paul failed to do, however, was correct
the abuses of Vatican II which, if anything, went from bad
to worse during his long pontificate. He was a papal power-
house who brought the Gospel to every corner of the globe.
And yet, his evangelical conservatism did not extend to
reforming the manner in which Christ was being made
present in the local church. Neither did it involve restruc-
turing priestly formation which was also in an alarming
state of disarray.[3] There are many possible reasons why this
was so, not least of which was the fact that the Pope had a
world historical vision which kept his eye firmly fixed on
the global rather than the local. But it is at the local level,
where the faithful congregate each day to worship, that
the future of the Catholic Church will be decided. To cite
Monsignor Gilbey once again: 'To make a true contribution
to putting the world right, we must first establish the
kingdom of God in our own hearts . . . The achievement of
sanctity is the complete fulfilment of each man's vocation.'

One individual who certainly recognized the truth of
that statement was Joseph Ratzinger. Contrary to those
who would say that the future Pope Benedict XVI was a
reactionary intent on dragging the Church back to the Dark
Ages, Ratzinger always maintained a great fidelity to the
reforms of Vatican II. He was after all an 'official theologian'

---

3   This, despite the fact that Pope John Paul wrote a truly magis-
     terial document on priestly formation entitled Pastores Dabo
     Vobis. See Pope John Paul II, Apostolic Exhortation 'Pastores
     Dabo Vobis' (25 March 1992), available at www.vatican.va.

or *peritus* to the Council, one who was, by all accounts,[4] one of its leading lights. And, as he subsequently wrote, it is 'impossible to decide *in favour* of Trent and Vatican I, but *against* Vatican II. Whoever denies Vatican II denies the authority that upholds the other two councils and thereby detaches them from their foundation'.[5] This enthusiasm notwithstanding, Ratzinger realized that the post-conciliar crisis in the Catholic Church stemmed from a misinterpretation and a misapplication of the Council's documents. Here is how the Cardinal, as Prefect of the Congregation for the Doctrine of the Faith, put it in 1985:

> What the Popes and the Council Fathers were expecting was a new Catholic unity, and instead one has encountered a dissension which – to use the words of Paul VI – seems to have passed over from self-criticism to self-destruction. There had been the expectation of a new enthusiasm, and instead too often it has ended in boredom and discouragement. There had been the expectation of a step forward, and instead one found oneself facing a progressive process of decadence that to a large measure has been unfolding under the sign of a summons to a presumed 'spirit of the Council' and by so doing has actually and increasingly discredited it.[6]

Does this mean that the Cardinal sought a restoration of what preceded Vatican II? That for him was never an option,

---

4   See Peter Seewald's impressive study *Benedict XVI: An Intimate Portrait* (San Francisco: Ignatius Press, 2008), and Vincent Twomey's 'theological portrait' *Pope Benedict XVI: The Conscience of Our Age* (San Francisco: Ignatius Press, 2007).

5   *The Ratzinger Report: An Exclusive Interview on the State of the Church* (San Francisco: Ignatius Press, 1985), p. 28.

6   Ibid., p. 30.

simply because the Church 'moves forward toward the con-
summation of history'. But what he did seek, and indeed
as pope still does desire, is 'a new balance after all the
exaggerations of an indiscriminate opening to the world,
after the overly positive interpretations of an agnostic and
atheistic world'.[7]

This excessive 'opening to the world' had a profound
impact on the very nature of Catholic identity. For many
Catholics, the Church was no longer perceived as the universal body of Christ, whose origins were not of this world.
By deviating so radically from the authentic texts of Vatican
II, the Church appeared to be a 'human construction, an
instrument created by us and one which we ourselves
can freely reorganise according to the requirements of the
moment'.[8] For a Catholic, however, the Church is that place
where heaven and earth intersect. It is, of course, composed
of people like you and me who, as Ratzinger says, 'organise
her external visage'. But behind all of this there is 'the
mystery of a *more than human* reality, in which reformers,
sociologists, organisers have no authority whatsoever'. If
it were only human, then everything, from the content of
faith to the liturgy and the sacraments, could be toyed
with on a caprice. Divest these things of their supernatural
dimension, in other words, and they become mere symbols
to be reinterpreted to suit the changing needs of each
context. Hence, in the aftermath of Vatican II, you had
priests exchange their sacred vestments for t-shirts, jeans
and sneakers; you had them 'consecrate' pizza bread, cook-
ies and cola; you had them corrupt the Eucharistic prayers
with their own bowdlerized versions – all of which they
did to the sound of popular songs. And even where such

---

7   Ibid., p. 37.
8   Ibid., p. 45.

desecration was not taken to those extremes, the sense of mystery, sacredness and awe which the Church and the liturgy are meant to inspire among the faithful, was squandered on an altar of inventiveness and 'originality'.

When seen as merely human, sacred things no longer exercise authority over those who worship them. It then becomes easy to play with the idea of breaking one's sacred vows or of defying official Church teaching. It then becomes easy for a priest to dismiss the idea that he stands *in persona Christi* (in the person of Christ), or for a parishioner to consider the Mass, not as a real confrontation with the risen Christ, but as a mere memorial of purely historical events. It seems to me that this is exactly what happened in the course of the decades which followed Vatican II. It seems equally obvious that the way to correct this is not to have more rupture, but to revive, in the spirit of genuine reform, the great traditions of the Church. This, once again, does not mean a restoration of the old order which preceded Vatican II. Neither is it a return to the claustrophobic Catholicism which characterized certain enclaves of the preconciliar environment. Rather, it invites us, in Ratzinger's words, 'to recreate an authentically Catholic climate, to find again the meaning of the Church as Church of the Lord, as the locus of the real presence of God in the world'.[9]

The first requirement, in so doing, is to recognize that the Church is not *ours* to do with as we choose, for ultimately it is Christ's church. This, of course, is not a sentiment which sits easily with the radical spirit. For to say that the Church is not ours, is not a purely human construct, but the manifestation of God's kingdom on earth – that is to reintroduce the idea of authority as a counterweight to

---

9   Ibid., p. 48.

unlimited freedom. But authority is not something which can be dispensed with if real freedom is to be realized. As that wise philosopher Hegel taught, real freedom is not anarchy, but the product of moral discipline and authority. We learn to value freedom only by recognizing its limits, and those limits are set by the people and institutions which surround the individual from birth. This means that I am not answerable only to myself, but to all those with whom I share the social space. Institutions serve, in other words, as the safeguard for genuine and durable liberty, in so far as they uphold the legal and moral norms which permit individuals to live in peace.

That rich concept of freedom, guaranteed by authority and obedience, was a major casualty of the misinterpretation of Vatican II. The aim was to proclaim that 'we alone are the Church' and that its traditional structures no longer command authority. This was, according to Ratzinger, 'a rejection of the concept of authority willed by God, an authority therefore that has its legitimation in God and not – as happens in political structures – in the consensus of the majority of the members of an organisation'. The Church is not in other words a political party, meaning that her structure is 'not *democratic* but *sacramental*'.[10] This is not to say that the people should be denied a say in how the Church is managed. Neither is it to suggest that it could survive without a proactive laity. It is simply to underscore the fact that, however vital the contribution of the laity may be, it does not *own* the Church. The Church belongs, first and foremost, to Christ as His body. This means that at its core, there is something immutable and unchanging, something permanent and everlasting. For Catholics, the

---

10   Ibid., p. 49.

primary purpose is not to alter the everlasting in their own image, but to alter themselves in the image of the everlasting. It is to genuflect in obedience before the sacraments as manifestations of God's grace and glory. Only then will it become obvious why the Church, even if it wanted to do, could never become a wholly 'democratic' institution.

When looked at in this way, reform of the Church can never equal revolution, which would amount to smashing the sacramental ethos of Catholic existence. Real reform, as explained by Ratzinger,

> is to strive to let what is ours disappear as much as possible so that what belongs to Christ may become more visible. It is a truth well known to the saints. Saints, in fact, reformed the Church in depth, not by working up plans for new structures, but by reforming themselves. What the Church needs in order to respond to the needs of man in every age is holiness, not management.[11]

This is a clear echo of Monsignor Gilbey's belief, that the cultivation of personal holiness must take priority over political programs. It is, however, a truth which fell foul of Vatican II 'reform'. Indeed, it is today an embarrassment for many Catholics to be publicly perceived as either saintly or holy. More significantly, many priests have long since eschewed the summons to saintliness, preferring instead to be seen as 'one of the people'. This has led, in turn, to the very proliferation of managers against which Cardinal Ratzinger warned. As I shall argue in more detail below, one of the most obvious consequences of the repudiation of the sacramental in favour of democracy was the emergence

---

11   Ibid., p. 53.

of a managerial class among the clergy. By shifting the emphasis away from the pursuit of holiness, the Church eschewed its traditional role as 'homeland of the soul' so as to assume the role of a social club. Where once it functioned as that site in which God and man could commune, it was now just somewhere to meet and play. Hence, in many places, the Parish Centre usurped the tabernacle as the focal point of Catholic consciousness.

As I see it, one of the root causes of the current clerical crisis is that priests have opted to become managers instead of saints. Where once they stood apart from the people in a spirit of sanctity, or as living symbols of the Incarnation, today they look and sound like administrators. In such circumstances, is it any wonder that so many of them lose their vocations or simply abandon their priestly vows? Listen once more to Ratzinger:

> The saints were all people of imagination, not functionaries of apparatuses. Outwardly, they were perhaps 'unusual' personalities, but nevertheless they were profoundly obedient and, at the same time, persons of great originality and personal independence. And the Church, I shall never tire of repeating it, needs saints more than functionaries.[12]

Only when the Church becomes rooted once again in saintliness and the sacramental, will it rediscover its true task in time. Only when it eschews the temptation to be a purely human institution, will it cease to be a bureaucracy characterized by priestly functionaries who have forgotten that their role is not to bring bingo to the people, but rather

---

12   Ibid., p. 67.

the crucified and risen Christ. Genuine renewal will only happen, in short, when both priests and parishioners realize what it is that Catholicism demands of them. In the first instance, it calls on them to seek Christ in the sacraments, and thereafter to imitate Him in their daily lives. This search for saintliness does not mean rejecting the world and all it has to offer. It is, to repeat what I said in previous chapters, a process of searching for salvation *in the midst of the world*, or in those places where we can be transfigured in Christ's image. This explains the vital significance of liturgical reform as a way of counteracting the worst effects of the hermeneutics of rupture.

This, once again, demands getting back to basics. When Vatican II permitted the use of the vernacular in the celebration of the Mass, it did so as a way of enabling ordinary Catholics to discover more bountifully its divine mysteries. The purpose, as can be clearly read in the Council texts, was never to change the substance of the liturgy itself. And that is because, like the Church, *the liturgy is not something that belongs to us*, or that we can refashion in our own image. If however you believe that the sacraments are *not* a manifestation of God in the corporeal context, then of course the liturgy – or the manner in which you celebrate the sacraments – can be changed to suit your particular taste. But Catholics *do* believe that these things are expressions of the eternal, and are therefore bound to acknowledge their constant character.

The sacred liturgy has what Ratzinger calls an 'unshakable' nature, one which cannot be creatively tampered with without sacrificing something fundamental. That is why Vatican II proclaimed in its great document *Sacrosanctum concilium*: 'Regulation of the sacred liturgy depends solely on the authority of the Church . . . Therefore no other person, not even a priest, may add, remove, or change anything

in the liturgy on his own authority.' In saying this, the
Council Fathers recognized that the liturgy should never
be characterized by clerical showmanship. Neither should it
involve shocks or surprise, or be a reflection of the times.
Being a living manifestation of the sanctity of Christ, the
liturgy is, in Ratzinger's beautiful expression, the 'common
homeland' for a Catholic, the very centre and 'source' of his
identity. He writes:

> Many people have felt and said that liturgy must be
> 'made' by the whole community if it is really to belong
> to them. Such an attitude has led to the 'success' of the
> liturgy being measured by its effect at the level of spec-
> tacle and entertainment. It is to loose sight of what is
> *distinctive* to the liturgy, which does not come from what
> *we do* but from the fact that something is *taking place*
> here that all of us together cannot 'make'. In the liturgy
> there is a power, an energy at work which not even the
> Church as a whole can generate: what it manifests is the
> Wholly Other, coming to us through the community.[13]

For the past 40 years, the Catholic world has indeed lost
sight of what is distinctive to the liturgy. Not only priests,
but also parishioners have traded its beauty and simplicity
for ugliness and utility. The liturgical constants which were
transmitted through the traditions of the Church have been
corrupted to the point where they are, in many instances,
no longer recognizable. If this has resulted in apathy, boredom and indifference, it is simply because, by squandering
that precious heritage, Catholics have forgotten what is
actually happening in the celebration of the Eucharist. They

---

13   Ibid., p. 126.

have lost sight of the fact that it is God, the Wholly Other, who becomes present to us in and through the liturgy. By this I mean that they no longer see with the eyes of faith, for that requires something more than what is 'comfortable and serviceable'. The Church has, during these decades, sought comfort when beauty should have been its goal. Instead of attempting to arouse 'the voice of the cosmos' and glorify the Creator, it has looked to the secular world for guidance and direction. And the result has been that the real reforms of Vatican II have been buried beneath an aesthetic wasteland.

To many modern ears, it might seem strange to say that the antidote to the crisis of Catholicism can be found in liturgical renewal. But if it appears strange, it is only because contemporary Catholics have little idea of what preceded this period of desecration. They have become so used to liturgical 'creativity' that they have all but lost touch with the Church's precious patrimony. Put simply: if Christ is today concealed from many Catholics, it is because one cannot truly encounter Him in the midst of what is ugly. Beauty raises us to God, and it is through beauty that He crosses the barrier separating the earthly from eternity. Consequently, it is a denial of Catholic identity to settle for anything less than the beautiful, the splendid and the majestic when worshipping Christ. Ratzinger goes even further when he asks: 'If the Church is to continue to transform and humanize the world, how can she dispense with beauty in her liturgies, that beauty which is so closely linked with love and with the radiance of the Resurrection?' No, he continues, 'Christians must not be too easily satisfied. They must make their Church into a place where beauty – and hence truth – is at home. Without this the world will become the first circle of hell'.

Is it a coincidence that when the Church decided to dispense with beauty, it fell into disarray? Is it a coincidence that when priests opted to offload beauty as too heavy a burden, many of them descended into that first circle of hell? It was, I wish to contend, no coincidence, simply because in rejecting the beautiful their eyes drifted from what is constant and eternal to what is transient and ephemeral. Hence the world and its seductions overpowered those senses which were once totally centred on Christ. Ratzinger agrees. For him, the big problem faced by priests and parishioners today is one 'of living without hope in an ever more profane world'. And, once again, the antidote to this is not more revolutionary reform in the direction of nowhere. Neither is it an even more 'secularized liturgy', but a new encounter with the sacred through a worship that manifests the presence of the Eternal'.

Beauty attracts. It elevates and ennobles all those who contemplate it. Without it, we feel alienated and isolated. If, therefore, the liturgy is a catholic's homeland, representing as it does man's fusion with his Creator, then it must be celebrated with all the majesty and solemnity we humans can muster. Otherwise, we fall far short of what it is to be Catholic. For Catholicism is a religion of beauty, one that considers the magnificent rites of the Holy Mass as the only appropriate response to the coming of Christ. Surrender that and the result will not be genuine renewal or reform. It will be, as Vatican II anticipated, nothing less than 'pastoral defeat' as the Church turns its back on 'the glory of God, the joy of faith, the victory of truth and light over error and darkness'.[14]

---

14   Ibid., p. 130.

4

From Boredom to Beauty

To put it in a nutshell: beauty matters to Catholicism because it is a religion which engages the senses. It is a sensuous faith which acknowledges humanity's deep need for aesthetic stimulation. Human beings are not self-contained, but desiring creatures who look beyond the ego for fulfilment. As Hegel put it, we desire to gaze upon the world to see ourselves reflected in it. A child, for example, acquires a sense of identity through building, making and creating. He seeks to bridge the divide between himself and the alien environment by interacting with it. In so doing, he leaves his mark or signature on nature, and infuses it with his consciousness or what Hegel called 'spirit'. Such is the process of *recognition*, whereby what was once different and potentially threatening is now recognized as one's own.

Catholicism never asks us to deny desire, for it understands that this would be tantamount to denying one's relationship to the world and to others. It recognizes that we are incarnate beings, and that it is through our bodies that we connect with creation. It is by virtue of our physical incarnation, in other words, that we attract and are attracted to others, and by means of it that we long to be at one (atonement) with those we desire and love. Hence the importance of beauty in Catholic worship, and the reason why Pope Benedict XVI sees the Church as that place where beauty and truth are at home.

Animals do not desire the beautiful. They are driven purely by instinct, and have no sense of what it means to crave something for its own sake. For that is what it means to contemplate something as beautiful: we see in it something which transcends the merely functional in favour of the eternal. When, for example, we ponder a beautiful person, painting or place, we do so not in order to see what it is that we can get out of it. On the contrary, to contemplate it *as* beautiful is to recognize that dimension of the thing which cannot be consumed or used solely to satisfy the self. The beautiful, in other words, is that which stimulates desire, but which refuses to succumb to it. It is that within the thing or person which signifies that it is somewhat set apart from the natural order. This explains why the senses cannot get enough of the beautiful and why our longing for it can never be completely satisfied. It is as if, in that moment when we encounter something splendid, the senses are saturated to the point of bewilderment. We long to possess that which we ponder, but complete possession proves impossible. Desire endures, that is, but never to the point of absolute fulfilment or exhaustion. While passion for the flesh may subside, infatuation for the beautiful persists undiminished.[1]

That is what I meant when I stated in the last chapter, that beauty elevates and ennobles all those who contemplate

---

1   For more on this, see Scruton's fascinating treatment of the beautiful in *Beauty* (Oxford: Oxford University Press, 2009). See also Chapter Three 'Gazing Aesthetically' of Mark Dooley, *Roger Scruton: The Philosopher on Dover Beach* (London: Continuum International, 2009), pp. 69–117.

it, and why Joseph Ratzinger continually emphasizes its deep connection with love. Love is best defined as desire for the beautiful, or desire transformed and turned in the direction of the transcendent. To love is to recognize that the object of one's affection can never be fully assimilated. There is always a surplus that exceeds the longing for carnal consumption, but which forever tantalizes and excites the emotions even in its absence. Indeed, it is not an exaggeration to say that without beauty there could never be true love. Without it, we would be stranded in a purely functional world where every desire and need would be fulfilled to the point of apathy and boredom.

It is this pivotal feature of the human condition which is reflected throughout the entire history of Church art and architecture. The great artists, composers and architects who contributed to that tradition, understood that nothing is more indicative of the human situation than our longing for the beautiful. And that is because, for them, this is ultimately a yearning for the sacred, the holy and the divine. What these people sought to do, however, was to define the indefinable, or to represent the true object of our love in figures that we could touch, hear and see. Needless to say, the result was only a partial representation of the ineffable. Still, it was nonetheless a glorious attempt to capture in concrete form that for which every human heart hungers. It was an attempt to put a face on love, and that face was, not surprisingly, the face of God.

Beauty restores us to harmony with the Divine – or at least as near to such harmony as we can get while still immersed in the flow of existence. It draws us from our earthly concerns so as to contemplate what lies on their other side. It offers us a glimpse, however incomplete, of eternity understood as the absence of temporality and desire. It presages, as such, that moment when all our striving, longing and pining will cease as we finally reach our heavenly home.

Now it is often claimed that Jesus, as a paragon of simplicity, would not recognize himself in the magnificent artwork of the Church in general, and the Vatican in particular. This inevitably leads to the suggestion that the Church should sell its artistic wonders in order to provide for the poor. My answer to that is simple: the Church holds its treasures in trust for the people of the world. Should it auction them off, the artistic inheritance of Europe would inevitably end up in the basements of the wealthy never to see the light of another dawn. Surely then, it is incumbent on the Church to retain these artistic treasures, each of which speaks of man's indomitable yearning to be close to Christ.

But there is something else which ought to be said: sacred art should not be condemned as either ostentatious or grandiose. As an illustration of man's unquenchable desire for God, it strives to bring heaven down to earth. It endeavours to overawe the senses with the power and majesty of Him who created the universe and who, as Catholics believe, fashioned humanity in His own image. That is why the works of Fra Angelico, Michelangelo and Bernini stun those who are lucky enough to savour them. For a brief moment, we are granted a glorious insight into what it will be like when that supreme object of human adoration will cease to be concealed by the Blessed Sacrament. In that instant, we have an inkling of how we will feel when our temporal sojourn ends and we return to the homeland of the soul.

Beauty is not, in other words, an optional extra when celebrating the Holy Eucharist. If anything, it is a material manifestation of our craving for Christ. It is an expression of our love for the Redeemer as revealed in the Bread of Life.

It is also a way of reconciling ourselves to the glory of God, a glory which inspires us to opt for the extraordinary over the banal. There is, however, another reason for why Catholicism seeks to adorn the Eucharist in beauty. I said above that Catholicism is a sensuous religion, in as much as it recognizes that we are not only spiritual but sensate beings. Our desires are intrinsic to who and what we are, and any attempt to suppress them is a denial of our humanity. This is not to say that desire cannot be correctly ordered, or that it is without a proper goal. What it does mean is that any account of the human condition which disregards desire is, at best, insufficient. It is no surprise, therefore, that the Eucharist fulfils both spiritual and corporeal needs. Our desire for Christ is, quite literally, sated through the physical consumption of His body and blood. But only *temporarily*, for the chasm separating eternity and time can be permanently bridged only in death. Hence the process of communing with Christ through the Eucharist is something which requires repetition.

Repeat something often enough, however, and it risks becoming a source of monotony. This is something that the exponents of the true spirit of Vatican II understood, and the reason why they have consistently called for continuity in the face of creativity. Liturgical beauty arouses the senses and heightens the desire for Christ. It is not merely an external embellishment, but a way of directing human consciousness towards the very core of the Catholic faith. Strip away the beauty of the sacred ritual, however, and you will only serve to desensitize people to the power and sanctity of the Blessed Sacrament. It is then that the ritual becomes routine, as desire for the eternal is diminished by an undue emphasis on the ordinary. But there is nothing ordinary about Christ – not if you believe He was God incarnate. That is why, in her ancient rites and traditions, the Church places heavy stress on aesthetics, or on *the way things appear*. Once again, there is nothing arbitrary in the way a priest vests for Mass; nothing random about the liturgical gestures; nothing accidental about the architecture of a well built chapel. All are ways of singing praises to God, and of bearing witness to the fact that our worship of Him should never be subject to mere human calculation.

This is why it profoundly matters what a priest wears, and why deviations from liturgical norms represent a repudiation of sanctity. I remember as an altar server in the 1970s, watching the old priests vest in the sacristy before Mass. These were men formed under the traditional rubrics of Vatican I, but who had embraced the authentic spirit of Vatican II. For these pastors, the priesthood was one endless prayer of thanksgiving whose summit was the Eucharist. Hence, they would arrive in the sacristy at least 15 minutes before the commencement of Mass, so as to properly prepare for their encounter with Christ. After a short period of silent reflection, or perhaps a rosary, the priest would proceed to wash his hands as a symbolic act of purification. He would then kiss the amice, or the white cloth which is conventionally placed around the priest's shoulders symbolizing salvation, and which acts as a shield against temptation. In so doing, he would recite a prayer asking that this 'helmet of salvation' protect its bearer from 'the assaults of Satan'. This was followed by the alb, or the white tunic which covers the body of the priest and which signifies integrity. Around the alb was fixed the cincture or a cord representing purity, after which came the stole which the priest wears around the neck symbolizing immortality and the dignity of the priesthood. Lastly, he placed upon himself the chasuble, or the outer garment whose colour is determined by the liturgical calendar, and which is worn, according to the Roman Missal, as 'an emblem of charity, which makes the yoke of Christ light and agreeable'. At each stage of vesting, the priest would reverently pray for Christ's grace to enable him to celebrate the Mass with appropriate dignity and respect for its sacred mysteries.

Each time I watched that beautiful ritual, I was brought to the edge of tears. Even as a boy, I recognized that the priest was not simply rehearsing an outmoded custom. He was binding himself to Christ in preparation for the Consecration. For him, those beautiful garments were more than just symbols: they were, as described by Pope Benedict, a reminder of the priest's 'transformation in Christ, and of the new community that is supposed to arise from it'. They are a challenge to the priest 'to surrender himself to the dynamism of breaking out of the capsule of self and being fashioned anew by Christ and for Christ'. Hence they contain a meaning which 'goes beyond that of external garments': they are 'an anticipation of the new clothing, the risen Body of Jesus Christ, that new reality which awaits us when the earthly "tent" is taken down and which gives us a "place to stay".'

If you want to know why the current pope places so much emphasis on the correct use of liturgical vestments, it is because they dramatically illustrate 'the purity and beauty of the risen body'. They remind us not only of the majesty of the risen Lord, but of the fact that the priest standing before us is not simply a man, but another Christ (*alter Christus*). As such, they indicate a thorough transformation of his person, one in which his temporal dimension is eclipsed by the eternal. That is why a sloppily vested priest, or one who arbitrarily decides to discard certain items of liturgical dress, is making much more than a fashion statement. He is, quite simply, refusing to 'put on' Christ – refusing, that is, to allow divine beauty irradiate his being so as to raise, in turn, the hearts of the faithful.

There is, in sum, a deep theological explanation for why a Catholic priest appears as he does on the altar, one which should never become the object of subjective manipulation. For when it is tampered with in that way, as it so often is in the contemporary context, the sacred beauty of the liturgy is compromised. Beautiful vestments are a glorious manifestation of Christ in the midst of the mundane. Hence no priest has a right to tarnish what the Pope's Master of Liturgical Celebrations calls, those 'holy signs which time has sifted, though which the Church speaks about herself, her identity and her faith'.[2]

If, therefore, the Holy Mass has become a source of boredom to so many, it is because the Church has been too quick to 'dispense with beauty in her liturgies'. It has been too quick to forget that the primary purpose of being a Catholic is to worship Christ in the Blessed Eucharist, and that if this is not emphasized in the way the Mass is celebrated, or in the way the Church is designed and decorated, then we can easily be tempted to forget about Christ. Everything in Catholic worship, that is, should tend towards the Eucharist. But if congregants are not consistently reminded of this, they risk lapsing into a state of indifference regarding the sacredness of the Holy Mysteries.

You cannot, in other words, dumb down Christ and expect that ordinary worshippers will continue to approach the tabernacle with awe. If their senses are not engaged by what they see and hear while in church, they will very quickly find a reason to stay at home. Inspire them, however, and the true meaning of the Mass will be made manifest.

---

2   From 'Introduction to the Spirit of the Litrugy', a paper delivered by Monsignor Guido Marini, Pontifical Master of Liturgical Ceremonies, to a conference for The Year of the Priest, Vatican City, 6 January 2010.

This, argues Pope Benedict, 'is no mere aestheticism, but the concrete way in which the truth of God's love in Christ encounters us, attracts us and delights us, enabling us to emerge from ourselves and drawing us towards our true vocation, which is love'. He adds: 'Beauty, then, is not mere decoration, but rather an essential element of the liturgical action, since it is an attribute of God himself and his revelation. These considerations should make us realise the care which is needed, if the liturgical action is to reflect its innate splendour.' This is something which even children can understand and appreciate. When, for example, I take my 5-year-old son to a hastily celebrated Mass, one in which the priest trades sanctity for showmanship, or one whose liturgy is characterized by kitsch, he soon gets bored and distracted. However, when he enters a church which, through its sacred splendour, opens wide the eyes of faith, he is completely captivated.

On one occasion, we attended the Solemn Mass of Corpus Christi which was followed, as tradition dictates, by a procession of the Blessed Sacrament. In this age of rupture, it is not unusual for such processions to be despoiled by priests refusing to wear the appropriate vestments, or by not following the liturgical rubric as recommended by the Church. But not, as it happens, on that particular day. From the moment the altar servers first emerged from the sacristy, it was apparent that this was not going to be, as Catholic commentator George Weigel might put it, *Corpus Christi Lite*. The altar was stunningly decorated in the correct liturgical colours. The chief celebrant was vested carefully and beautifully. Incense was used at the appropriate moments of the Mass. The hymns sung were of the timeless variety, each conveying a deep sense of sacredness. And when, at the end of the procession, the choir performed a glorious rendition of the greatest of all Eucharistic hymns, *Pange*

Lingua by St Thomas Aquinas, followed by an even more beautiful *Salve Regina*, the congregation could barely contain its emotion. It was then that my little son, who, of his own volition, fell to his knees during the *Pange Lingua*, turned to me and said: 'Can we please come here every week?'

The reason why the pews of that particular church remain packed, notwithstanding the current crisis, is simply because its clergy refuses to trim the liturgy to the times. They understand that people do not come to Mass to focus on each other or on the priest, but to focus exclusively on their Lord. It is imperative, therefore, that the space in which Christ appears be kept sacred. This is reflected in the care and attention which the priests of that parish pay to maintaining the sanctuary and the shrines which surround it. It is also reflected in the fact that many of the old devotions which have long since disappeared from many parishes, have been retained and are flourishing. This suggests that contrary to the 'creative' spirit which seized the post-Vatican II context, most parishioners do not want the Mass to be a group therapy session. They do not want it to be a sing-along affair where congregants sit around holding hands. They go to church to be reminded of the majesty and saving power of their Creator, He who 'shows us how the truth of love can transform even the dark mystery of death into the radiant light of the resurrection'. They go because they want to experience 'something of that beauty which Peter, James and John beheld when the Master, making his way to Jerusalem, was transfigured before their eyes'.[3] They go in the expectation of feeling what my son felt as he spontaneously

---

3   *Sacramentum Caritatis*, Post Synodal Exhortation on the Eucharist of the Holy Father Benedict XVI (Catholic Truth Society, 2007), p. 38.

blessed himself before the Sacred Host, to the haunting strains of 'Sing, my tongue, the Saviour's glory (*Pange lingua gloriosi*)'.

At its best, Catholicism understands that how we build is not a matter of personal taste or interpretation. It recognizes the deep philosophical truth that architecture directly affects the way we live and how we relate to others. Hence it cannot be subject to endless experiment for, as Roger Scruton explains, it is an expression of 'the human determination to dwell in a place, not for a day or a year; not even for thirty years, but forever'.[4] Church architecture traditionally reflected this quest for permanence and sacred origins. Indeed, for Scruton, the human urge to build can only be truly understood in religious terms. Like the liturgy, the temple 'is forever', its stone being 'the earthly translation of God's immortality, which is in turn the symbol of a community and its will to live'.[5]

Most churches built over the past 30 years were, however, designed in defiance of this truth. By borrowing on contemporary architectural trends which rendered them purely functional, they came to symbolize the very essence of the spirit of rupture. Externally, many resemble community halls, warehouses, or, in one particular case that I know of, a swimming pool. In some instances, they bear no sacred signs, not even a Cross. Internally, they look like poorly planned theatres, the emphasis having been removed from the tabernacle and placed squarely on the 'actor' leading the drama. The intention in such cases was to lend credence to the prevailing 'revolutionary' view, that these

---

4   Roger Scruton, 'Classicism Now' in Mark Dooley (ed.), *The Roger Scruton Reader* (London: Continuum, 2009), p. 166.

5   Roger Scruton, *Perictione in Colophon: Reflections on the Aesthetic Way of Life* (South Bend: St. Augustine's Press, 2000), p. 90.

places were certainly not an earthly translation of God's glory. If anything, they were built as a defiant statement to the effect that the liturgy is not 'God's summons to His people to be in His presence'. Their purpose was not, as Pope Benedict remarks, to 'reawaken the interior sense of the holy', but to force people into conceiving the liturgy 'as an object, the property of man'.

The temple, in short, is supposed to restore us to God. It is supposed to be the place where all members of the great eternal society can commune. It is supposed to covey a sense of tradition, of the everlasting and of our potential to transcend death. It is, moreover, supposed to be a place of silence and meditation on things which are not of this world. In essence, it is supposed to be a satellite of heaven here on earth. That is why, in the old chapels, everything is directed towards the tabernacle – that place where the Sacred Host is solemnly retained. Everything, that is, points away from self and towards God. In these splendid structures, we are reminded of the sacrifices of the saints, and are summoned to pay homage to the martyrs by lighting a flame before their shrines. We are aware that in these places, the dead can always find rest among the living. For here, there is a heightened consciousness of our fragility, and of our dependence on forces which far exceed our capacity to contain. And most of all, there is a peace which surpasses all human understanding, and which refreshes both body and soul in equal measure.

Conversely, in those churches which are the product of modern architecture, the focus is taken off God and put on the people. In such places, you do not sense the eternal since you are forced to stare at your fellow-congregants and, most especially, the celebrant. Indeed, as monuments to modernity, such churches champion rupture over reform and critique over continuity. Their purpose is to sever the congregation from the pursuit of timelessness, so as to fix their eyes on the fleeting. Upon entering such structures, it is not unusual for people to experience disorientation, ultimately resulting in a loss of spiritual purpose. Where once the church was a concrete expression of a changeless liturgy, one which centred the lives of believers on Christ, it is, in such cases, a denial of divinity. The idea is not to elevate the soul in the direction of eternity, but to drag God from His heavenly pedestal and place him where he belongs: at the back of the room.

A striking illustration of this is to be found in a prominent 'oratory' here in Ireland. The gaudy tabernacle is at one extreme, the wooden altar is in the middle, while the ambo (the stand from which the Gospel is proclaimed) is at the far end of the oratory. The congregation is seated – for there is no provision to kneel – on chairs which face each other across the room. Neither is there any provision to pray before traditional icons, given that all the artwork is bordering on the New-Age. In short, this oratory is designed in such a way that the people 'pray' toward each other, which they must do either from a sitting or standing position. The building dictates that you shall not adopt a conventional liturgical rhythm, and that your actions be divested of their Christly orientation. People in this context are not God-focused, but *other-focused*. The community becomes what the Pope aptly calls 'a self-enclosed circle', one which 'no longer opens out to what lies ahead and above, but is closed in on itself'.[6] And when that happens, as it has so often in recent Catholic history, priests and parishioners can easily forget the precise nature of what it is they are

---

6   Joseph Cardinal Ratzinger, *The Spirit of the Liturgy* (San Francisco: Ignatius Press, 2000), p. 80.

ultimately doing. It is then that they begin to see the Mass, not as the source and summit of Christian life in which God draws us to Himself, but as a simple community service.

There is, to repeat, a deep symbolic reason for everything that is characteristic of Catholic worship, which is why it is not only a religion of beauty and wonder, but also one of meaning. There is a reason why, for example, the altar should never be placed in the centre of a congregation, but ideally should face towards the East. For when the altar is located at the centre surrounded by the congregation, we lose that sense of expectation for the Wholly Other. We turn our back, as it were, on the Lord. But when people and priest face east, they tend in the direction of Jerusalem, knowing that together they are 'in a procession toward the Lord'.

Now this does not mean, as was so often the case in the pre-Vatican II context, that the altar should be remotely positioned from the people. But it does mean that it be situated in such a way that it inspire a common form of worship towards He who is to come. What is imperative is that the focus be deflected away from the priest in the direction of the crucified and risen Christ. Having been eclipsed by Christ in his vesting, the priest should seek to stand aside as the gateway to paradise opens at the Consecration. In that sacred moment, all eyes should be on the Eucharist, and they should be the eyes of faith. This helps explain why, when it not possible to face east, the Pope recommends that a Cross be placed at the centre of the altar. In this way, says Benedict, 'we look together at the One whose death tore the veil of the Temple – the One who stands before the Father for us and encloses us in his arms in order to make us the new and living Temple . . . Is the cross disruptive during Mass? Is the priest more important than the Lord? This mistake should be corrected as quickly as possible; it can be done without further rebuilding. The Lord is the point of reference'.[7]

All of this means that when a church serves a purely functional purpose, when it fails to reveal the beauty of the risen Christ through its shape and structure, the point and promise of Catholicism is radically obscured. No longer is it a place where worshippers can experience homecoming, permanence and eternity, for what it represents is a repudiation of tradition, taste and the timeless. The implicit message in contemporary church architecture is that, as a community, we stand alone perpetually severed from our origins. Hence the emphasis is on *us* in the here and now – the self-contained community divorced from the eternal society.

This is no less true of much modern church music. Once again, the purpose of sacred song is to open a space for the coming of Christ. It is to sing His praises and to convey a sense of the heavenly realm to which the liturgy invites us to belong. Indeed, of all the arts, music is the most spiritual, liberating as it does the emotions from their physical entrapment. Consider, however, the differences separating sacred from contemporary music. The first seeks to glorify God through harmony and melody. The music, like the Spirit, enters the soul of the listener and binds it to those angelic voices which seem not of this world. But it also testifies to a great musical tradition which includes composers like Palestrina, Byrd and Schubert, all of whom correctly conceived of beauty as being next to Godliness. For them, there is nothing more important that a human being can do than worship the Saviour, which is why, when music is employed to serve that purpose, it must be nothing short of glorious.

---

7   Ibid., p. 84.

Now compare that tradition to pop. The principal purpose of pop is not to lift its listeners heavenwards. If anything, it is to liberate the body from the bondage of authority, responsibility and sacrifice. By moving to its artificial beat, the followers of pop are possessed by a spirit of rupture which rejects homecoming and identity for alienation and discord. This, of course, is not to claim that contemporary musical genres cannot be successfully deployed in a religious context. The success of the folk movement, of Taizé, and of the uplifting spiritual anthems used during the World Youth Day celebrations, provides ample evidence of their power to provoke prayer. But when it comes to the celebration of the liturgy nothing can replace those timeless hymns which, to use Scruton's phrase, are born from the 'sacred form of life', and which seamlessly evoke the enormity of what is happening. This explains why, conventionally at least, the organist and choir are positioned on the balcony at the rear of the church. In this way, the emphasis shifts from the performers to the music itself, from the source of the song to its goal which is to focus its listeners on the beauty, mystery and dignity of the Eucharistic celebration. And in so far as the great sacred hymns are drawn from an ancient patrimony, they allow us to sing in harmony, not only with the angels, but also with our ancestors.

If boredom and lethargy have consumed the Catholic faithful, it is I believe because they are settling for far less than they deserve. They are trying to mould something sacred into something mundane, and the result is just what you might expect: the great mystery around which Catholicism turns has become lost in an ocean of distractions. Instead of gazing in awe at their Creator, Catholics, either by choice or circumstance, are shifting their sight elsewhere. But, as I have been suggesting, there is a way of

71

restoring focus. Priests and parishioners must look beyond themselves, beyond Church politics and scandals, to those simple yet splendid avenues along which Christ reveals Himself in time. They must reignite their desire for a liturgy steeped in beauty. In so doing, the true power of the sacraments will become apparent, as will Christ's sublime divinity revealed in His Body and Blood. And the proof of that lies in the fact that in those parishes where this is recognized as a reality, there is no crisis or mass exodus of the faithful. There is simply a longing for that precious moment when, each Sunday, the Holy Mass is celebrated in the full glow of its intrinsic beauty, and when, at its end, the 'little ones' turn and ask: 'Can we please come here every week?'

5

What It Means To
Be a Priest

In the wake of the awful clerical child sex abuse scandals, I was asked by my editor at the *Irish Daily Mail* to write a column on some controversial comments made by the Archbishop of Dublin, Dr Diarmuid Martin. In a speech delivered to the Knights of Columbanus in May 2010, the Archbishop claimed that there were 'strong forces' within the Church 'who would prefer that the truth did not emerge'. He did not say who these forces were, but he did stress that the cause of the crisis was due in part to a 'culture of seminary institutions which produced both those who abused and those who mismanaged the abuse'. I found this extraordinary because, as I wrote in my article, 'for the very first time, a senior member of the Irish hierarchy has laid some of the blame for what happened to children under the care of the Church', on the way Irish priests are formed. It had always seemed obvious to me that if priests were betraying their sacred vows – if they were dumbing down the liturgy and trading purity for the profane, there was something dysfunctional in the way they were being trained. I had no doubt, in other words, that the culture of rupture had not stopped short of the seminaries, and that if true reform were to be achieved those institutions had to be thoroughly investigated.

As it happens, I was in a good position to make that demand. I had taught for some years in the Philosophy Department of the National University of Ireland at Maynooth (NUIM), which is also the setting of the National Seminary, St Patrick's College. Clerical students were obliged to attend my philosophy courses at NUIM, and as the years progressed I became aware that many of them were deeply dissatisfied with seminary life. And so, when Dr Martin identified seminary formation as part of the problem, I decided to speak publicly about the challenges facing prospective young priests in Ireland and, as I would soon discover, elsewhere across the world. Here is a sample of what I wrote:

> While it is true that only a very small percentage of priests were responsible for the horror visited upon countless innocent children, it is also true that the Irish Church has not, more generally, been blessed with great pastors. I have visited innumerable parishes in recent months, and the story is invariably the same: priests have little theological or intellectual clarity. Their sermons are slight and shallow. They speed through the Mass at lightening pace, display little reverence during the Consecration, and give Communion as though handing out fliers at a concert. And all that because, as Dr Martin expresses it, they have forgotten that 'the Church is fundamentally a worshipping community founded in and nourished by the Eucharist'. Or is it that this message was never sufficiently inculcated during their training? Let me tell you why I ask this question.
>
> The most promising clerical students I have taught are not promising because of their training, but because

they have modelled themselves on truly great priests. Indeed, I can disclose that these young men consider the prevailing culture of the seminary to be less than satisfactory. For example, the most devout students are often sidelined. In some cases, they are invited to consider whether they really have a vocation. In other instances, they are simply asked to leave. If you find that strange in an age when priests are at a premium, you are right. What it suggests is that a cosy clerical cartel still controls the seminaries. And if a courageous young seminarian should dare challenge that culture, he will soon find that his future as a priest is in doubt. Why is that? Why is it that my best clerical students over the years are those who have been made to feel most uncomfortable in the seminary? And why is it that they must look beyond the seminary to find the inspiration they are searching for? Once again, the answer is to be found in Dr Martin's wise observation that the Church is 'founded in and nourished by the Eucharist'.

A priest is not meant to be a social worker in a collar. Neither is he supposed to a committee chairman, a counsellor or a manager. He is above all else an *alter Christus*, or another Christ. The priest is, in other words, the means by which Christ reveals himself to man in time. Through his hands, the Bread of Life is consecrated, and another more heavenly world opens up to the faithful. He is the portal through which the Divine light shines on both the righteous and the sinner. That, at any rate, is how many of my young clerical students perceive the true role of the priest. And yet, it seems that such a definition of the priesthood is not only rejected by what Dr Martin labels 'the narrow culture of clericalism', but worse, they consider it an embarrassment. In order to 'fit in', such clerics no longer want to stand out, and so they simply deny who and what they are. As one very fine priest put it to me recently, 'many of them simply don't believe in what they are doing any more'. In such circumstances, is it any wonder that parishes are no longer vibrant centres of evangelisation? Is it any wonder that people, young and old, are drifting from the Church in order to find spiritual satisfaction elsewhere? And is it any wonder that, as the Archbishop decries, there are 'very few pastoral initiatives to reach out to young people'?

I do not say that the only path to renewal of the Irish Catholic Church is by taking 'a radical new look at the formation of future priests'. But it is, as the Archbishop suggests, one of the most important routes. And that is so, because it is only when the priest recognises his role as that of *alter Christus*, that the Church will rediscover its true vocation as a 'place where we encounter the love of God revealed in Jesus Christ'.

Put very simply: parishioners do not want counsellors in collars. They want men who will, in deep sanctity, put them in touch with their saviour each Sunday. They want to witness the Word made flesh, and they want it consecrated in beauty. This means that they want their churches to be places where the pulse of eternal life never ceases to beat, and where the priest devoutly fulfils his role as that point of intersection between this world and the next. This begs the obvious question: would the catastrophic crisis currently affecting the Irish Church have happened if, over the past few decades, Irish seminarians had been correctly trained? It seems to me, as it does to the Archbishop and those courageous clerical students who are the true future of Irish Catholicism, that you could not be moulded as an *alter Christus* and abuse anyone, least of all a child.

That is why both Dr Martin and Pope Benedict are correct in pointing a stern finger of blame in the direction of Irish seminaries. It is also why, as demanded by the Archbishop, 'the narrow culture of clericalism has to be eliminated' in order to revive the Church's 'prophetic role in society'. But if this is to be genuinely effective, it must also involve listening and learning from those disenchanted young seminarians who must daily live with the rot, and yet who still believe passionately in the priesthood. In so doing, the Irish Church will have a real future – one led by those for whom the call to follow Christ is not a source of shame, but the very essence of their lives here on earth.[1]

That column triggered a tidal wave of interest. In the days following its publication, I received hundreds of letters and emails from priests, seminarians and ex-seminarians, thanking me for shining a light in places where only darkness had hitherto prevailed. So overwhelming was the response that I decided to use my weekly column in the *Irish Daily Mail* to highlight just how bad the seminary situation had become. Entitled 'Sin within the Church is born in Seminaries', this column sought to synopsise the heartbreaking accounts which flooded across my desk in the wake of my first comment on the matter:

I am not in the habit of writing this column in anger, for nothing stymies moral clarity more than senseless fury. But there are times when anger is morally justified, such

---

1   Mark Dooley, 'There are Dark Forces in the Church and They're Ruining its Chances of Survival' in *Irish Daily Mail* (5 May 2010).

as when we encounter injustice or corruption. Even Christ, whose message of love is the cornerstone of Christianity, could not restrain his rage when he discovered the desecration of the temple in Jerusalem. We in Ireland are currently witnessing a similar, if not much worse form of desecration. As I wrote in this newspaper last Wednesday, Irish seminaries are hotbeds of serious moral decay which is devastating the Church in this country. Their culture is one that rejects piety and holiness in favour of religious laxity and moral confusion. This is resulting in priests who, as I wrote, barely believe in the doctrine they are ordained to promote.

Once again, in other words, the temple has been hijacked by those who Christ banished from its courts. This time, however, they are not in the business of changing money and selling doves, but of prostituting their priestly principles to an ideology which runs contrary to their faith. That is the source not only of my anger, but of the deep frustration felt by scores of seminarians who must live with this problem while preparing for the priesthood. I know that, not only because I have had the pleasure of lecturing some of them over the past number of years at NUI Maynooth. In recent days, I have also been inundated with letters of support from many more who found my article to be a source of comfort and consolation. These are courageous young men who, like me, believe that the seminary system is the fundamental cause of the Church's crisis. As one seminarian put it, 'if Ford has a problem with cars, there is only one place they go to root out the fault: the factory'. The Pope knows this, which is why he said *en route* to Fatima this week that the greatest threat to Catholicism 'is born of sin within the Church'. That sin begins to fester at the moment of formation, and has the potential to destroy some priests and the unfortunate parishes in which they are placed.

Very few who enter the seminary system stay the course. According to one individual, of the fourteen who started in formation in 2009, only eight remain. Why? Not, as you might imagine, because they revealed themselves to be lacking in sanctity. In many cases, it was because they were deemed too devout. Another seminarian passionately laments that he is not allowed to kneel during Mass. In the course of his studies, certain 'priestly' professors have informed him that there is 'no such thing as transubstantiation [the conversion of the bread and wine into the Body and Blood of Christ], and that he should not look to Rome as 'they don't know anything'.

Worse still is the fact that those who wish to uphold the old devotions, such as the Rosary, are frowned upon. All are taught that the Eucharist should not be taken literally, but is a mere 'memorial' of an historical event. This means that the Holy Mass should be interpreted, not as the moment when Christ crosses the barrier between time and eternity, but as a simple 'gathering' of the 'community'. Those who object are either sidelined or shown the door. Those, in other words, who consider the priest an *alter Christus*, or another Christ, are driven from its potential ranks, or made to suffer for the sin of simply longing to make manifest their Lord. Meanwhile, others whose lifestyle is a travesty of the priestly life are made to feel at home. How on earth can the Catholic Church in Ireland recover when the very people charged with training our future priests are doing such damage? It seems perfectly obvious to me that the only way you are going to counter this catastrophe, is by forming priests in the image of Christ. But that, to their great shame, is precisely what Irish seminaries are refusing to do, seeing it as a retrograde step. That is why the 'apostolic visitations' promised by Pope Benedict in his recent pastoral letter to the Irish people, cannot happen too soon. And they must begin right at the heart of the rot, in those places which punish the pure and reward the reckless. They must start by listening to those brave former students of mine, who have had to live in fear for simply wanting to imitate Christ.[2]

---

2   Mark Dooley, 'Sin within the Church is Born in Seminaries', *Irish Daily Mail* (12 May 2010). Following the publication of these columns, the *Irish Daily Mail* commissioned an independent investigation into the state of Irish seminaries. Published under the title 'An Unpriestly Education', it confirmed and substantiated most of my claims. Here are some of its findings: 'Seminarians who piously follow the tenets of the faith are belittled, they claim, while those who follow the more liberal approach, encouraged by visiting psychologists and counsellors, flourish in the liberal environment . . . Even more astonishingly, the pervasively sexual atmosphere at the college – where relationships thrive and where allegations of abuse routinely are made light of, even dismissed out of hand – is mirrored by a drinking culture that largely is ignored, setting a pattern for future alcohol dependency among those who have opted for the celibate life . . .

Certainly, for one seminarian, who we shall call Paul, the gulf between what he expected from his vocation and what he experienced was vast. 'We were initially greeted by a director of formation, who was a priest, before we commenced the first month in seminary known as a spiritual or introductory month,' he explains. 'Initially, the talks and group discussions were bland and riddled with pop psychology, but nothing scandalous occurred until we were launched into a sexuality workshop, led by lay women, that lasted several days.' 'The reality of mortal sin was rejected and all sexual acts, regardless of their nature, were regarded as equally valid and lawful . . .' 'What was disturbing was that the basic principles of the moral life were turned on

It was then that I began receiving messages of support from across the Catholic world. Clerics wrote me from

---

their heads. Rather than being encouraged to conform our passions to the will of God, the feeding of the passions, specifically the sexual passion, was considered the ultimate end. This was disturbing to many of us, principally because we believed it contravened the law of God.' 'News reports about paedophile priests were nothing new at this stage, and it was quite obvious that these horrific acts were the result of a process where the sexual passion was not controlled, but fed . . .'

For another seminarian, Peter, disillusion was almost instant. 'I had been warned by friends of a culture of spying and intimidation inside the seminary system, where things you confided in other students would be repeated to you by priestly members of the so-called Seminary Council. 'It is widely known that, each year, some second-year students are requested to return early from the holidays to show the new seminarians the ropes. Their main function, however, is to gather information on what the first-years are saying and doing. The information they possessed was quite incredible – some were even able to inform us of who was going to be kicked out.'

Nor did the curriculum match any of Peter's expectations. 'When you enter a seminary, you might think that those charged with formation would ask if you went to daily Mass, were you a regular attendee at Confession, were you loyal to Church teaching and, most importantly, whether you truly believed Jesus Christ was God. Not once was I asked these or similar questions.' 'You also expect to be taught the Catechism and encouraged to read the Bible. Again, not once was I encouraged to do so during my time at the seminary.' But if no questions were asked about inner belief, nor was there much outward evidence that students were in a seminary at all. 'You would expect to find a crucifix displayed in each study room, the bedrooms, the offices of the priests in charge, or at least some kind of religious symbol or picture,' says Peter. 'But there was nothing of the kind.' The heavy emphasis on sexuality also unnerved him. 'We were asked regularly how we controlled our sexual temptations,' he says. 'We could not understand this, as we believe it is a grace

Britain and the United States expressing similar concerns, and saying that their experiences mirrored those of my own students. I learned that my articles had been read with interest by senior members of the Roman Curia, one responding that 'this Dooley business does not surprise me at all. The only surprise is that it has taken so long to bring it to public attention'. But what struck me most was the response of ordinary Catholics to what they were reading. All were supportive and appreciative, but that was tempered

---

you receive from God and hence not an issue for those who pray about it.'

For Luke, who also left the seminary for a religious order more in step with his own faith, the main shock came in the teaching of the gospels. 'The Bible was divested of all its supernatural dimensions,' he says. 'According to this "interpretation", Jesus did not perform miracles or dispossess people of evil spirits.' 'I heard one senior priest comment during a homily that those people exorcised by Jesus were not in fact possessed, but merely suffered from a form of psychological illness.' 'Due to an erroneous interpretation of Vatican II, the "presence" of Jesus in the Blessed Sacrament is widely rejected. If true, this would of course completely undermine a priest's reason for being.' 'As far as I could see, the Mass had turned into a simple memorial service, completely bereft of its true sacrificial or supernatural character. No wonder then that one priest was frequently seen chewing gum during Mass . . .'

'What amazed me was that a significant number of the priests we encountered not only dissented from official Catholic doctrine but appeared to support ideals which are in defiance of Papal teaching,' Peter says. 'The Mass is not considered the holy sacrifice of Jesus on Calvary, but a community meal during which some priests were seen to alter the Church's Eucharistic prayers by inserting their own words and phrases. We were not allowed to kneel at the Consecration and I can remember that the few students who insisted on kneeling did not last very long in seminary life'. (*Irish Daily Mail*, 17 July 2010)

by a great sense of disbelief and distress, as poignantly summed up by one Irishwoman:

> Thank you for having the courage to let us know what is happening in our seminaries. Do our bishops know, or care, and if they do why isn't something being done to help keep our fine young and faithful men in the priesthood – men that we need so badly. My hearts gets so heavy. I feel so sad for our beautiful faith and our beautiful Mass.

I profoundly empathized with that woman, because what I had revealed struck me as a betrayal of the priesthood itself. In their enthusiasm for the culture of creativity, those charged with training future priests had sought to undermine the very essence of the consecrated life. In their desire for novelty and originality, they had sought to sacrifice saintliness for a priesthood rooted in its opposite. And the dire consequences of this were dramatically apparent on almost every altar across my country. The priest had become a clerical counsellor, one for whom the affairs of this world were all-consuming. He desired so hard to blend in that he failed to fulfil his true vocation, which is to stand *in persona Christi* (in the person of Christ). Indeed, the contemporary seminary culture frowns upon this goal, which it deems too 'outdated' for a modern priest. Hence the reason why so many priests refuse to celebrate the Eucharist in beauty and sanctity: thanks to their training, they believe that to so do would distance and alienate them from their parishioners.

That, however, is contradicted by those priests who refused to retreat from holiness in the manner suggested by their seminary superiors. According to some very fine clerics who wrote in support of my findings, the seminary system was just as bad in the 1970s and 80s. Those men only survived because they longed to imitate Christ. This meant looking beyond the seminaries in order to emulate those priests who embodied the old theological virtues which once animated the priestly state. As I say, Catholics do not want their priests to blend in, but to stand out. That is why Pope John Paul II, despite his counter-cultural pronouncements, was so revered by the young. Like the saintly Pope Benedict, he appeared to be in the world yet not entirely of it. It seems perfectly evident to me that if priests were trained along those lines, there would be no crisis of faith, no crisis of vocations, and no crisis of clerical abuse. For how could those who truly stand *in persona Christi* betray anything, least of all their sacred vows?

To be 'another Christ' means learning to let go of self. It means banishing ego in order to assume the mantle of the Good Shepherd. This requires a programme of formation which puts candidates on the path to holiness. It does not demand putting them in touch with their feelings, or making them into spiritual social workers, or training them as functionaries. If anything, it demands teaching them the value of saintliness in a world where it is all too uncommon. I said in the previous chapter that nothing undermines the sanctity of the Eucharist more than a sloppily vested priest, or one who does not treat it with due reverence. That is so because, as mediator of the Divine, the priest is supposed to serve as a living icon of Christ. He is supposed to be a resplendent reflection of heavenly radiance in the midst of all that is otherwise. This means that when the faithful look upon a priest celebrating the Holy Mass, it should be like standing in St Peter's shoes at the foot of Mount Tabor during the Transfiguration. What we should see is someone glowing with light from another sphere – someone for whom the concerns of this world have been eclipsed by the splendour of the next. And when we bask in that glow, it follows that we cannot but be fully conscious of Christ. We cannot fail, that is, to be touched by the sight of someone for whom saintliness is not simply an aspiration but a concrete reality.

When a priest conforms himself to Christ in this way, when he celebrates the Mass in beauty and sanctity, he serves as a magnet to the faithful. For it is then that they feel a true connection to Christ, one inspired by the priest's inspirational example. In holiness, the spirit is elevated heavenwards so that the Eucharist becomes a tangible expression of eternity. To say that this is all parishioners want from their priests is not an exaggeration. Today, the Catholic laity is a highly educated body. Indeed, many of them are better educated than their priests. They do not go to church for lessons in pop psychology or political reflections on our duty to the environment. They go to meet with Christ in the Blessed Sacrament, an encounter which they expect to be the highlight of their week. But thanks to the poor quality of priestly formation over the past 40 years, their expectations are rarely realized. For what they now behold on the altar, is not another Christ but *another self*, one who appears to be doing a routine task rather than one attempting to pry open the gates of paradise.

Priesthood is not a job but a state, one which must be cultivated from the moment a candidate first walks through the gates of the seminary. It involves prayer and penitence, both of which serve to purify body and soul. It involves trading one's civilian clothes for priestly garments and vestments. And it does so, not for the purpose of decoration, but because they symbolize a detachment from the world and its pleasures. They signify that the prospective priest is shedding his temporal skin so as to put on Christ. That is why it is a travesty of priestly formation to abandon the old conventions in a spirit of rupture and discontinuity. It is a travesty to deny seminarians their right to say the Rosary, to wear their cassocks or to spend their free time in Eucharistic adoration. For how else are they expected to become truly centred on Christ, and how else are they supposed to become conscious of the fact that theirs is an entirely new state of being? How else, in other words, can they aspire to holiness if they are deprived of the only means through which it becomes manifest?

There are those who will say that this vision of the priesthood is not the answer to, but the cause of many of the Church's problems. They will argue that the crisis stems in large part from the pompous piety which once personified the priesthood, and which merely served to distance pastors from their parishioners. They will add that this model must be shelved and replaced by one which fully embraces the world, and which puts the priest back in touch with his person. This will naturally involve abandoning celibacy which, they say, is the real source of clerical sex abuse.

My response to that is twofold. First, if a priest is totally rooted in Christ, he will neither be pompous nor distant. The whole point of a Eucharistic priesthood is that the priest is so moved by love of God, that he naturally extends this love towards the neighbour. Indeed, he is more likely than most to understand what such love requires and the sacrifices it involves. For, as Pope Benedict XVI wrote in his first encyclical *Deus Caritas Est*: 'Worship itself, Eucharistic Communion, includes the reality both of being loved and of loving others in turn. A Eucharist which does not pass over into the concrete practice of love is intrinsically fragmented.'[3] Stay rooted in the vine, in other words, and

3   See Encyclical Letter, *Deus Caritas Est*, of the Supreme Pontiff Benedict XVI (25 December 2005). The Encyclical is available in full on www.vatican.va.

'you will remain in my love'. But when the priest is severed from the root, when he prefers all that human to that which is holy, it is then that he is tempted away from service and back to self. It is then that he will seek to satisfy himself before saving the other in a spirit of saintliness.

Secondly, it is simply not credible to argue that celibacy is the cause of clerical child sex abuse. Once again, if a priest steadfastly stands *in persona Christi* he could never entertain the possibility of abusing anyone. That is why most priests would rather die than abuse a child. Having transfigured themselves in the image of Christ, they have, in turn, sublimated their sexual desires in the pursuit of holiness. It is, moreover, a terrible insult to all those who have consecrated themselves to Christ, to suggest that their sacrifice is a recipe for sexual deviance. For the fact remains that the vow of celibacy did not make once-perfect priests into paedophiles. In reality, paedophiles who had no intention of upholding their vow of celibacy, managed to become priests. And, as it happens, the majority of them did so precisely at a time when the spirit of creativity was seizing control of the seminaries. Put simply, when priests are genuinely formed in the person of Christ, as indeed they once were, the sexual urge is transmuted into a desire to serve both God and neighbour. And when that happens, as one seminarian put it to me, 'you understand the beauty and worth of selflessness'.

This is all by way of saying that the priest should not be a manager, a bureaucrat or an administrator. He is there to bring Christ to the people in a manner befitting such a transcendent task. The big mistake, as I see it, was to think that tampering with his identity as an *alter Christus* would make him into a better priest. But that is the idea which took hold of those charged with training future priests in the post-Vatican II era, and which has contributed in no small way to the current seismic crisis in Catholicism, including the dearth of vocations. This was something which struck Archbishop Elden Curtis of Omaha back in 1996. In an article published that year, he wrote:

> I personally think the vocation 'crisis' in this country is more artificial and contrived than many people realised. When dioceses and religious communities are unambiguous about ordained priesthood and vowed religious life as the Church defines these calls: when there is strong support for vocations, and a minimum of dissent about the male celibate priesthood and religious life loyal to the Magisterium: when bishop, priests, religious and lay people are united in vocation ministry – then there are documented increases in the number of candidates who respond to the call.

The Archbishop adds that the crisis is, in large part, 'precipitated and continued by people who want to change the Church's agenda, by people who do not support orthodox candidates loyal to the magisterial teaching of the Pope and bishops, and by people who actually discourage viable candidates from seeking priesthood and vowed religious life as the Church defines these ministries'.[4]

As I endeavoured to highlight in my dispatches on seminary life in Ireland, little has changed since Archbishop Curtis wrote those words, a view confirmed by American author Michael Rose in his recent groundbreaking book

---

4   Archbishop Elden Curtis, 'Crisis in Vocations? What Crisis?', originally published in *Christian Order* (March, 1996). This article is available in full on www.ewtn.com.

Goodbye Young Men.[5] Rose writes that while the dramatic decline in vocations across the United States (39, 638–4, 826 between 1966–1999) has been blamed 'on a multitude of factors including materialism, practical and philosophical atheism, scepticism, subjectivism, individualism, hedonism, social injustice; parents who don't want their sons to be priests; and the commonly perceived "unrealistic expectation" of lifelong celibacy', the real reason is just as Archbishop Curtiss suggested: it is one of 'ideological discrimination' against those candidates who aspire to stand *in persona Christi.* And it is this, more than any other factor, which has contributed to the liturgical catastrophe which has become such a pervasive feature of contemporary Catholic life.

Put simply, renewal of the priesthood must start by restoring to the seminaries and the churches, that venerable old vision of the clerical disposition. This is something which Pope Benedict clearly understands, which is why in May 2010 he appointed the Archbishop of New York, Timothy Dolan, as Apostolic Visitor to the seminaries of Ireland. Archbishop Dolan is a widely read columnist, blogger and an exquisite communicator. But he is also a man of immense good humour, something which he sees as vital for revitalizing the priesthood. As he says when discussing seminary recruitment: 'Happiness attracts'. Those are not the words of a detached idealist, but of one who speaks from direct experience. When he was appointed as Archbishop of Milwaukee in 2002, Dolan was confronted with a massive sex abuse crisis involving 58 clergy. He was also successor

---

5   Michael S. Rose, *Goodbye Good Men: How Liberals Brought Corruption into the Catholic Church* (Washington: Regency Publishing, 2002).

to a bishop who, as he says, 'resigned in ignominy after revelations that he had paid an adult male partner $450,000 of archdiocesan funds'. Still, he handled that terrible affair with great skill and sensitivity, while simultaneously focusing on seminary formation. Not surprisingly, seminaries once again began to flourish under the Archbishop's direction. I say 'not surprisingly', because Timothy Dolan has written what I consider to be the finest book on the priesthood in print. *Priests for the Third Millennium*[6] is a beautifully crafted, witty and inspirational account of the form priestly life ought to assume in the modern age, one which he summarized in a speech to faculty and staff of St. Patrick's College, Maynooth, shortly after his appointment as apostolic visitor.

In that speech entitled 'God is the Only Treasure People Desire to Find in a Priest', the Archbishop exhorts priests to 'recapture holiness'. 'Might I propose,' he says, 'that what sparks and sustains sanctity is the Holy Eucharist. The daily celebration of the Eucharist, with proper preparation, joyfully, sincerely, reverently offered, the anchor of a day laced with prayer, from our morning offering to our *Salve Regina*, especially that prayer which is such a constant of our life that we priests call it our office, is the key to intimacy with Jesus, which is *holiness*'. All else flows from a Eucharist which is celebrated with enthusiasm, joy and deep reverence – a Eucharist that grounds the priest in 'daily intimacy with Jesus', and thus with his neighbour. As he writes, the Eucharist 'is where we experience our priestly identity most intimately. Is there ever a more powerful moment of configuration with Christ, of acting *in persona Christi*, than

---

6   Timothy M. Dolan, *Priests for the Third Millennium* (Huntington: Our Sunday Visitor Publishing, 2000).

when we say, "This is my body; this is my blood?" We are Christ!'[7]

In a world where it is routine for priests to rush through the Eucharistic prayers, where Elevation of the Host and sacred Chalice lasts but a second, it is rare to hear a cleric speak so passionately and lovingly about that moment when he places us in Christ's presence. But the Archbishop does precisely that, because he is 'configured at the core of his being to Jesus Christ as head, shepherd, and spouse of His Church'. For him, the priesthood is 'a *call*, not a career; a *redefinition* of self, not just a ministry; a *way of life*, not a job; a *state of being*, not a function; a permanent, lifelong *commitment*, not a temporary style of service; an *identity*, not a role'. In other words, a priest's value lies not in what he does, but in what he *is* – in his *being* another Christ. And that is not because 'doing, actions, ministry, service' are not important, but simply because 'unless what we do flows from who we are, we're shallow, empty functionaries'.

Who would choose a functionary when he could have Christ? Who would choose a social worker when he could have someone who has the power to transmit the treasures of heaven? Who wants the Mass to be downgraded by a pastor who only belongs to the Church, as Archbishop Dolan puts it, 'for power, authority, privilege, or entitlement'? That is 'clericalism, and it is a vice, a sin', and it is so because the only thing Jesus asked of His followers was 'to *remain* with Him, to *abide* with Him, to *rest* with Him, to *come* away with Him, to *stay* with Him, to *keep vigil* with Him'. And what of those who think that such a programme for priestly renewal is 'overly pious and simplistic',

---

7   Ibid., p. 234.

or those who think that 'being *grounded* in *holiness* is not enough in an emergency so desperate'? To such people, Archbishop Dolan simply says: 'It is no more simplistic than the exhortation given us by the Master Himself, "Seek ye first the Kingdom of heaven and all else will be given thee".' And 'to those who wonder if holiness, humility and identity are a pollyannaish ignoring of deep psychological turmoil in the priesthood, I say with Adrian van Kaam, no, as a matter of fact, *holiness* means wholeness, and wholeness means integrity, and a man of integrity hardly abuses our youth or overlooks the crimes of those who do'.

Great priests like Archbishop Dolan demonstrate that the Holy Mass, celebrated in sanctity, is all Catholics need to be fulfilled. Indeed, nothing else should matter. For it is there, at the heart of this ageless ritual, that we encounter the Creator. That is why it needs to be celebrated by good and holy men – people for whom the Eucharist *is* life. Get the right priests, in other words, and the sacred source of our redemption will be revealed in all its splendour. Get the right priests and there would be no need to ask the question: 'Why be a Catholic?'

6

What It Means To Be a Parishioner

If the liturgy is the 'homeland of the soul', the place where God and man become one, then it must serve as the pivot around which all else hinges. To repeat: everything we need from Catholicism is supplied in the Mass. What happens in the Parochial House, or the Parish Hall, is insignificant when compared to that moment each day when the priest elevates the sacred Host saying: 'Do this in memory of me'. In that instant, when the light of heaven pierces the sacramental bread, Catholics are nourished in every conceivable way. Now it may be, thanks to the problems of the priesthood which I discussed in the previous chapter, that they do not always experience the true significance of that moment. But profoundly significant it is, and when celebrated with due reverence it cannot but replenish a hungry soul.

That is why it counts as a source of curiosity to me, when it is suggested that the problems of the Catholic Church can be solved through increased lay involvement in the liturgy. For two years, I served as Chairman of a Pastoral Parish Council. It was an enriching experience which gave me an insight into the workings of daily parish life. But one constant refrain from parishioners was that in the laity lies the future of the Church. My reaction to this was that while the laity certainly has a vital role to play in the passage of sacred history, enhancing its role still further, especially in liturgical matters, will certainly not counter the troubles of Catholicism. This was usually greeted either with stony silence or incredulity, for it has become an article of faith among certain sections of the lay faithful that only they can provide a panacea to the Church's ills.

My proposed solution is not one which seeks to exclude the laity, but one which *redirects its focus*. The Catholic laity, I argue, has become so involved in parish life that the lines of demarcation between it and the priest have, in many cases, all but disappeared. In fact, so involved is the laity in some contexts, that all they are short of doing is saying Mass. But this, we should note, has done nothing to either prevent or stem the crisis in the Church. In saying this, I do not mean to suggest that there is no place for Ministers of the Word, of the Eucharist, or for all those who so worthily give of their precious time in order to enhance the Mass. What I am saying is that while this has undoubted value, it is not going to remedy the situation in which Catholics now find themselves.

While there is, in other words, a need for what Vatican II calls 'active participation', there is an even greater need for what Pope Benedict terms 'authentic participation'. This means that there is a requirement on each Catholic to fully participate and engage in the Eucharist, for it only there that the mysteries of faith can be authentically experienced. 'Participation' in this context, implies cultivating a 'greater awareness of the mystery being celebrated and its relationship to daily life'.[1] Following the instruction of Vatican II's *Sacrosanctum Concilium*, it suggests that parishioners should

---

1   Pope Benedict XVI, *Sacramentum Caritatis*, p. 49.

participate in 'the sacred action, conscious of what they are doing, actively and devoutly'. And they should do so, not because they need to 'know their place', but because it is only through *authentic* participation that the true purpose of the Mass, and thus of Catholicism, can be rendered luminous and meaningful.

Whenever I give a public talk on this subject, it always strikes me how few Catholics understand what is going on during the Mass, even among those who actively participate. There is, for example, very little understanding of why the liturgy takes the form it does, why certain vestments are worn at certain times, and of the underlying significance of the sacred symbols. If there is, therefore, a pervasive sense of apathy regarding the Mass, it is because its true beauty and meaning has been sacrificed to ignorance. At a time when there is more active participation than ever, there is virtually no authentic participation. The consequences of this cannot be underestimated. For when parishioners become desensitized to the sacred drama which unfolds during the Eucharist, they simultaneously become disconnected from the 'life of the Church as a whole, including a missionary commitment to bring Christ's love into the life of society'.[2] When they fail to understand that the purpose of parish life is not committee work, councils or fundraisers, but what happens in the church itself – it is then that they lose sight of what it truly means to be a parishioner. They lose sight of Christ as He reveals Himself through the Host, thereby depriving the self of its sacramental sense.

Once again, it is difficult for many to accept that the source of parish renewal is a better knowledge of, and a deeper devotion to the Mass itself. But this, I suggest, is

---

2   Ibid., p. 52.

only for the reasons I gave in the last chapter: many priests, seized by the 'creative' spirit, refuse to let the true beauty of the Eucharist shine forth. In so doing, they diminish it to a lifeless burden which serves only to alienate and disenchant parishioners. If, however, the Mass were celebrated as it should be, it would be seen as a constant source of 'sacramental empowerment', one through which our actions are conformed to those of Christ. At that point, the distinction between what worshippers do and the *actio Christi* (the activity of Christ) disappears. Listen again to Benedict XVI: 'There is only *one* action, which is at the same time His and ours – ours because we have become "one body and one spirit" with Him. The uniqueness of the Eucharistic liturgy lies precisely in the fact that God Himself is acting and that we are drawn into that action of God. Everything else is, therefore, secondary.'[3]

The primary objective of Catholic worship is the *actio Christi*. As with the priest, who should ideally seek to surrender himself to Christ during the Holy Mass, so the parishioner ought to have only one aim: to reconcile his life to that of the Saviour. The purpose, to repeat, is not to focus on the priest or on each other, but on the One who invites us to eat His flesh and drink His blood. The purpose is therefore atonement and communion with the source of eternal life, which means following the priest in shedding self so as to permit the Spirit take possession of the parishioner. This cannot happen, of course, if the Mass has been voided of its intrinsic beauty and solemnity. Neither can it happen if the celebrant fails in his calling as an *alter Christus*. For it is then that the longing for salvation is stunted by banality and showmanship.

---

3   Joseph Cardinal Ratzinger, *The Spirit of the Liturgy*, p. 174.

Ideally, priest and parishioner should be related dialectically, suspending their temporal concerns so as to raise the heart heavenwards. But this can be achieved only when their gestures mirror the *actio Christi*. For that is what the Mass fundamentally is: an invitation to bend body and soul towards the sacred. It is a summons to become another self in Christ. Authentic participation requires that from the moment we step inside the sacred space, we tend towards the Lord. It demands a purification of self in order to respond appropriately to the sacramental and salvific character of the moment. It cannot, as such, be preoccupied solely with the external rhythm of the liturgy. The beauty of the outwards signs is but a means to raise the congregant's consciousness to God, leading ultimately to full communion with Him. This, in turn, effects a complete conversion of the person, so that from the church the parishioner goes forth in a Christ-like spirit of charity and goodwill.

I first learned of the importance of the *actio Christi* from my grandfather. As a young boy, I often accompanied him to the local church where he served as a money collector. But for him, collecting the offerings was simply a sideshow, one which he did as an act of devotion to the Church. It was participation of an active kind, and one which could easily get in the way of its authentic counterpart. And so, as we approached the chapel in our finest clothes, he would encourage me to closely observe and imitate the movements of the congregation as they partook of the liturgy. This, he made clear, was not a set of empty gestures, but nothing less than a supreme act of consecration to Christ. It was an outward expression of an inner transformation, which not only won for the penitent a place in paradise, but enabled him to live a happy and holy life. The result was that what initially seemed, to my tender eyes, as strange practices, had now become a visible manifestation of humanity's longing for the invisible.

Upon entering the church, my grandfather would thus pause, dip his hand into the Holy Water font and lovingly bless me. He would then invite me to make the sign of the Cross as a pledge of loyalty to the Crucified. He taught me to do this tenderly and with extreme care, making sure that I never construed it as a sign of shame. It was, he said, a seal against danger and temptation, an emblem of honour which would keep me alert to my better angels. But it was also the best way to sanctify a person in preparation for the Holy Mass. It was as if, in anticipation of the Resurrection, the body was being wrapped in the burial cloth of Christ.

From there, we entered the sanctuary and genuflected before the tabernacle. I always admired the manner in which my grandfather genuflected. He did so gracefully and with much love. Slowly, he would bow his head before dropping to the floor on one knee, a position he would solemnly maintain for some seconds. Here was an old man, the *pater familias*, surrendering all his strength to the Lord. For him, this was not a sign of weakness, but an act of submission to his Maker. Eventually I learned to emulate this action, and to recognize that bearing public witness to Christ is not a choice for a Catholic. It is an obligation which defines who and what we are.

That is why, if he were alive today, my grandfather would weep at the sight of parishioners bypassing the Holy Water font, bowing instead of genuflecting, or, in some instances, simply refusing to acknowledge the tabernacle as that which reserves the risen Christ. He would do so because, for him, those simple actions were acts of thanksgiving for the benediction we were about to receive. They were the only suitable response to what he considered to be the spiritual acme of human existence. They were, in other words, a small sacrifice to pay for the privilege of being in His presence.

My grandfather took very seriously Christ's call to lose one's life in order to save it. And he believed that we could achieve this through authentic participation in the Eucharist. Through the *actio Christi*, he thought, we can become a new self. But this means sacrificing all that is merely human in honour of the sacred, which we can experience only in silence. Sacred silence is not dumbness, for communication with Christ often takes the form of a conversation. But it does involve silencing the mouth in favour of an interior dialogue. While we are required to verbally respond at various junctures during the Mass, we do so in prayerful solemnity aware that our words are directed elsewhere.

For my grandfather, the real enemy of such Eucharistic prayer was babble. Nothing offended him more than the sound of casual conversation in a church, for this was to drag the world into a place where it simply did not belong. Not only does it prevent proper preparation for Mass, but it ensures that those who wish to pray cannot. Obviously, this is a real danger at the beginning and end of Mass, but it has, more recently, become a feature of the period following Holy Communion. And when that happens, the possibility of becoming a new self in Christ is lost. To be in conversation with others at the very moment when silent communion is called for, is to lose that redeeming sense of the sacred. It is to interrupt the Host as He offers Himself up for our salvation.

In silence I am conformed to Christ, for it is then that I can truly listen to His Word and respond with generosity. And when I am invited to speak it is not simply to fill the void, but rather to sing His praises and declare one's faith. This suggests that authentic participation eschews activity, if by that is meant movement (verbal or physical) which distracts from the *actio Christi*. That is why, for my grandfather, the more time spent on one's knees during Mass the better. As with genuflecting, kneeling was not for him an expression of servility. It was a humble act of submission to the Saviour from whom all good things flow. It was, once again, a way of bending the body to Christ – an admission that before Him we are nothing, and that ours is a completely dependent state. It is also, as my grandfather often reminded me, the way Jesus prayed to His and our Father. Such is my reason for being dismayed when I enter those churches which make no provision for kneeling, and also why Irish seminarians are currently so anguished about being denied their right to kneel before the Blessed Sacrament.

In the sacramental world occupied by my grandfather's generation, kneeling at the moment of consecration and communion was central to their Catholic identity. In both cases, you were in the presence of Christ, and no other action was considered appropriate. My grandfather felt so passionately about this, that I discovered him on bended knee before the television as he watched Pope John Paul II celebrate Mass in Ireland in 1979. At that moment, he may not have been actively participating in the papal liturgy, but he was authentically participating. Like Pope Benedict, my devout old granddad understood that the 'man who learns to believe learns also to kneel, and a faith or a liturgy no longer familiar with kneeling would be sick to the core'.[4]

By the time he arranged for me to serve Mass, my grandfather had instilled within me an insatiable love for

---

4   Ratzinger, *The Spirit of the Liturgy*, p. 194.

the liturgy. He spent much time explaining that serving Mass was not a simple matter of assisting the priest: it was nothing less than serving Christ. In his simple yet wise manner, he taught me that the liturgy was not up for grabs, that it could never become the object of manipulation. For these are, he insisted, 'timeless things', the fruit of His agony, death and resurrection. And when treated as such, they have the power to make of someone a saint.

My grandfather never claimed to be a saint, but in his pursuit of holiness through the sacraments, he personified the virtues of a true parishioner. In so doing, he never felt the need to become a Minister of the Word or the Eucharist, for that, he believed, was to tread on sacred soil which should be occupied only by those who were ordained. It was enough for him to pass the collection baskets, for that was work which any person could do. Anything else would be a distraction from becoming a new self in Christ, which was, for him at least, the real objective of leading a Catholic life. In this vein, he urged me to see the church as a stepping stone into another world. Even when alone in such a place, you are surrounded by the spirit of the saints. By following the Stations of the Cross, you can walk with Jesus to Calvary. By kneeling before the tabernacle, you can enter His real presence. Indeed, it was he who first enlightened me to the fact that the church is the gateway to that great eternal society, into whose sacred depths only the eyes of faith can peer.

On a sharp winter's night in 1982, my grandfather was struck down by a stroke which stripped him of his physical and verbal powers. Until his death in 1986, he would never again visit the church which provided him with so much spiritual solace. As we processed into his beloved parish chapel on that sad day, I noticed that standing on the altar were some priests who had not served in the parish for many years. They returned, I later learned, because, as curates, they had been moved by my grandfather's example of dignified piety. For them, his love of Christ, as exhibited in his devotion to the liturgy and the Church, was an inspiration. It could not be said that he was particularly active in the parish, but he was a truly authentic witness to his faith, one for whom participation meant penitence, purity and prayer. And that was apparent to everyone who experienced him kneeling in silent adoration at the foot of the altar, or to those who observed his awestruck demeanour during the Consecration of the Mass. As a young boy, I marvelled at the sight of this old man unashamedly offering his strength and soul to a God made present in the simple form of bread and wine. I marvelled also at how he would leave the church possessed of an inner joy which radiated from every pore of his being. In turn, that joy would translate into acts of love and kindness, not only to his family, but also towards those he met socially and professionally. Most especially, it was evident in the way he loved his grandchildren, and in how he fostered in me an abiding fascination for the sacramental and its redeeming strength.

My grandfather did much to put the world right, as Monsignor Gilbey might have said. But he did so not by serving on committees or councils, or by 'actively participating' in the liturgy. Rather, he did so by establishing the kingdom of God in his own heart, the result of which was the 'achievement of sanctity'. For this, he sought no acclaim or recognition. He simply wanted the Mass to structure his existence, and to let whatever divine energy he received from it, shape his character and relations with others. He was, thus, a genuine Catholic role model – a living testament to the power of the old religion to elicit holiness from the heart of humility.

But he was not the only one. My boyhood world was dominated by people who believed that if priests did what they were supposed to do, and parishioners did likewise, there could never be a crisis of faith. If priests stood *in persona Christi* and parishioners imitated the *actio Christi* – if, in other words, the Eucharist became the source and summit of their existence – then the beauty and richness of Catholicism would always serve to inspire saintliness and convert even the most cynical. This means that being Mass-focussed is to be Christ-focused, and being Christ-focused is to be transformed in His likeness. It means that the 'real "action" in the liturgy in which we are all supposed to participate is the action of God Himself'. It is the 'deed of God, and for that very reason the liturgy of faith always reaches beyond the cultic act into everyday life, which must itself become "liturgical", a service for the transformation of the world'.[5]

If the liturgy is no longer perceived as such, if it is losing its transformative power, it is not solely due to a hunger for rupture among certain elements of the Catholic clergy, or to bad priestly formation - although that is, as I have argued, a significant cause of the crisis. It is also because people like my grandfather are a dying breed. As a child, I was not schooled in the theology of liturgy or in advanced catechesis. But thanks to my grandfather's example, I knew what it meant to authentically participate in the Mass, and the profound effect that could have on a life. Being surrounded by people like him, I did not have to ask what the purpose of the sacred signs, symbols or gestures was. I simply observed those penitents in prayer, and the answer shone like a beam through the night sky.

---

5   Ratzinger, *The Spirit of the Liturgy*, p. 175.

From a distance, I now know that most of those people were, in their own quiet but cheerful way, authentic examples of sainthood. For them, parish life was nothing less than participation in the life of Christ. And that was all the participation they required to make themselves into earthbound icons of His heavenly love. As such, they would have undoubtedly agreed with Pope Benedict when he remarks, that true 'liturgical education cannot consist in learning and experimenting with external activities'.[6] For what it demands is an interior form of martyrdom, in which one's old self is crucified only to be resurrected in Christ. And this is something that you cannot learn from books, or by serving on councils and committees, but only through the faithful witness of those who still believe their parish to be a source of divine grace.

---

6   Ibid., p. 175.

7

Solace in the Sacraments

One morning in 2006, a student asked if he could speak with me in private. Obviously anxious and in need of guidance, he told me that for many years he had been in psychotherapy but was still consumed by anguish. His problem, he explained, was an abiding sense of guilt which he simply could not shake. He was unable to pinpoint the source of the guilt, but no matter what he did the torment refused to retreat. The years of therapy had left him penniless, but had done nothing to assuage his anxiety. He had talked much about his parents, his siblings and his sexuality, but never about his spirit, his soul or the sacred. Those things were, for his therapist, the stuff of superstition, as much to blame for his condition as any other factor. Indeed, the primary cause of his shame and guilt was, according to the counsellor, the Catholic culture in which this man grew up. It had, she claimed, stunted his sexuality and made him subservient to a 'Father' who would never recognize him for the man he was. For that, according to most models of psychoanalysis, is what the Catholic God is: a heartless guardian who demands that we renounce our personal freedom in order to win his favour, and which even then may not be forthcoming. He is a God who calls for sacrifice and renunciation, but one who refuses to reward those who surrender to his requirements. The answer, therefore, is not to punish the self for the sins of the Father, but simply to repudiate him. This means rejecting 'family values' and any other device which serves to force us into submission. It means 'castration' and 'circumcision', to use the therapeutic jargon, from the supposed origin. It means, as I said in the first chapter, rejecting somewhere in favour of nowhere.

Week after week, my student lay on his therapist's couch in pursuit of a cure which never came. At the end of each session, he was informed that much more work needed to be done before healing could be had. He was told that only liberation from his past would enable him to find peace, the first step towards which was to study the great 'masters of suspicion' from Nietzsche and Freud to Sartre and Foucault. But the writings of one individual in particular were prescribed as a solution for all his problems: R. D. Laing. Laing believed that only by liberating the 'true self' from the forces of oppression, could it realize its proper potential. And what exactly are those forces? According to Laing, 'families, schools, churches are the slaughterhouses of our children; colleges and other places are the kitchens. As adults in marriage and business, we eat the product'.

In other words, all those institutions which provide peace, security and settlement are, in the eyes of the Laingian therapist, the locus of personal disorder and moral decay. My student's therapist instructed him to follow Laing by turning his back on 'the norm' in order to embrace 'transgression'. This meant alienating himself from family and friends, from his religion and his relationships. The result of this 'inner revolution' was not, however, the promised euphoria, but even more intense feelings of guilt, disquiet and despair. Meanwhile, the endless therapy sessions continued to take their toll on his pocket, and ultimately on his health.

After confiding all this, my student then paused and said: 'It is years since I have been to confession, but it is slowly becoming clear to me that it alone can provide the real "talking cure".' Here was a man immersed in a therapeutic culture, one where every secret is exposed in the form of TV and radio confessions, as well as on email and Facebook, and yet he felt more alone than ever before. He had dozens of virtual friends, but no real friends. Each week, he opened his soul to a woman who responded with neither guidance nor support. And then, quite suddenly, it began to dawn on him that what he needed was not mental or physical therapy, but spiritual healing. He knew, of course, that I was a Catholic, but also one who had given serious study to the history of psychoanalysis. He knew, in other words, that I had experience of both the couch and the confessional, and that I would therefore speak with conviction about why I had repudiated the former in favour of the latter.

The first big difference between the couch and the confessional, I explained, is that while the couch costs, the confessional is a gift. Like everything else that Christ bequeathed to man, the sacrament of reconciliation is offered without expectation of return. It is a gift of grace that those ordained *in persona Christi* can give to any soul in search of spiritual succour. And all it requires is that the individual display true penitence for sin. Sin, of course, is something which few will today acknowledge. Like guilt, it is dismissed as yet one more tool in the service of supernatural superstition – a hangover from a pre-Freudian picture of the human condition. In truth, however, it is still the best way of understanding our insuperable need to conquer estrangement and alienation. The reality of sin reminds us that we are dependent beings, and that we require the love and forbearance of others to survive. We need others to excuse our faults and to look with mercy upon our transgressions. Most of all, we need to know that, even when such human forgiveness is not forthcoming, it is available in abundance from the heavenly Father. We need to know, in other words, that there is always someone who will love us despite our weakness and our failings, someone who will simply say the word and we shall be healed.

Sin and guilt are not, as Nietzsche argues, the source of our slavery, but the very basis of morality itself. Like shame, guilt enables us to recognize when we have transgressed too far, and thus when reparation is required. Without guilt, in sum, we would never know, or care, when the moral law has been contravened. We would never know when our actions and ambitions have served to thwart those of the neighbour. That is why a guilt-free culture is both dangerous and threatening: by lifting the claim which the moral law makes upon the self, the ego is then free to pursue its pleasures without consequence. Having escaped the manacles of psychological suppression, it need not sacrifice its desires in order to accommodate those of others, or humble itself in the face of accusation and blame. Neither does the ego feel the need to seek forgiveness, for it denies that rights and entitlements should always come second to sacrifice and responsibility.

Catholics see things very differently. For them, there is nothing oppressive in answering the claim which guilt makes upon the self. They recognize that we are not free-floating egos, but mutually reliant beings with an insuperable yearning for reconciliation and atonement. We want to be at peace with both ourselves and our neighbours, a peace which is the principal source of real freedom. For it is only when personal and social harmony is restored, that we can proceed unburdened by the weight of the past. Put simply, Catholicism is a religion which prioritizes the other. It is a religion which defines the human being as a responsible agent, one whose rights are guaranteed only through its adherence to duty. But it also recognizes that the force of the ego is strong, and can, at any time, seduce a person into turning his back on the neighbour. It is then that humility gives way to arrogance, and shame gives way to sin.

The couch can and does offer a lot of things, but what it cannot provide is a lasting cure to that fundamental human temptation. Indeed, its stated purpose is not to 'cure', for that presupposes that there is a 'normal' state to which we can be restored. But normality, at least for most modern forms of analysis and therapy, is code for power and oppression. Hence the aim is to break man's chains so that he can embrace 'authentic' freedom. Still, at one level, the therapeutic process is not unlike the Catholic sacrament of reconciliation. There is a confessional, a confessor and someone seeking comfort – except that the therapist is not there to heal, but simply to facilitate. And because the unconscious is multi-layered, the process has the potential to drag on *in perpetuity*. Not so with Catholic confession. As often as people require it, they can find immediate reparation, and thus the peace which surpasses all understanding. Not only can they experience inner restoration, but they will also be reconciled to those against whom they have trespassed. For that is the essence of this beautiful sacrament: it is a divine font of forgiveness which provides a fresh start for shattered souls.

The confessional stands before the penitent as a symbol of Christ's limitless mercy. It is a concrete sign of the gift which He poured out for mankind on Calvary. It is not there to humiliate, embarrass or subjugate. Its only purpose is to wash clean all those whose humility draws them to its threshold. Unlike a therapy session, where analyst and patient are positioned face to face, the Catholic priest is shielded from the penitent. In darkness, and from behind a grid, he sits in silence as the individual lists his sins, unburdens his soul, or simply tells his sorrowful tale. And then, after some gentle words of consolation, the *alter Christus* asks the penitent to undertake a small act of penance, before inviting him to declare his contrition before the Creator. This is followed by the highpoint of the Rite of Confession – that moment when the redeeming waters of eternity cleanse, absolve and purify. Holding high his hand in preparation for the final blessing, the priest prays: 'God, the Father of mercies, through the death and resurrection of his Son, has reconciled the world to himself and sent the Holy Spirit among us for the forgiveness of sins; through the ministry of the Church, may God give you pardon and peace, and I absolve you from your sins in the name of the Father, and of the Son, and of the Holy Spirit.' No other words supply more solace and consolation to people in spiritual pain. In a matter of seconds, the weight of one's past drifts away, leaving the penitent free to resume his life in love and joy. And, once confessed, those sins are gone forever: no more worry, no more fear, no more despair.

As I explained all this to my student, he vowed there and then to trade the couch for the confessional. What followed was quite remarkable. After years of seemingly endless agony, he joined a queue of people waiting to kneel before the Father of mercies. In those moments, he felt more at one with himself than he had in a decade. He watched as fellow-penitents emerged from the confessional cleansed of their woes, their faces shining with what was to him an unfamiliar serenity. As his turn approached, he simply kneeled and prayed for assistance. His confession lasted ten minutes, and then he heard those heartrending words: 'I absolve you from your sins.' Nothing prepared him for the eruption of emotion which followed. Here was someone who had become enslaved to the past, and now, in the twinkling of an eye, it was no more. The Father of mercies had immersed this suffering soul in the blood of his Son, and in that instant he was reborn. Anxiety gave way to relief, depression to delight, and rejection to complete acceptance of his life and all the blessings it contained. Through the darkness of the confessional, the light of life irradiated his existence and made him high on hope.

Such is another wonderful example of the sacramental character of the Catholic life. From the moment of birth, Catholicism offers the comfort of Christ through the gift of the sacraments. By way of oil, bread and wine, we are drawn into a community bound together by the One who sacrificed Himself for our salvation. The sacraments are, as such, the product of sacrifice and surrender. They are loaded with love, signifying as they do the selfless agony of the Cross. And what they offer, as He promised, is rest for all those who labour and are burdened. My student was burdened to the point of paralysis, but he found rest in that little box wherein life, no matter how damaged, can be instantly refreshed and renewed. He found mercy, for-giveness, tenderness and compassion, to the point of being overwhelmed. And that, in turn, enabled him to live and love once more.

No therapist has the power to pardon a person. But a Catholic priest can do so, not by virtue of his own power, but because he acts *in persona Christi*. Catholics believe that in confession they are speaking directly to Christ. As in the case of the Holy Eucharist, the priest is but a mediator between God and man. That is why it really does not matter to whom the Catholic confesses. For, once he enters the confessional, the penitent is not kneeling before another mortal, but before the Creator. But this in turn demands that the priest be of the utmost moral and spiritual probity, and that he conforms himself as closely as possible to Christ. Otherwise, there is always the risk that the priest's own ego will come between the penitent and Christ, thereby shattering the trust upon which the entire process is predicated.

I say this because I know first-hand how deeply disturbing it can be for a penitent to have his trust in the confessional undermined. For some years, I confessed my sins to an individual who I believed was a model priest. He celebrated the Eucharist with great reverence, preached with passion and conviction, and appeared to live a faultless existence. But then, one Sunday, I picked up a newspaper only to read that this same priest had been removed from active ministry due to allegations of sexual impropriety. Nothing can prepare a person for such a shock. This was a man to whom I had opened my soul, and who had responded with wise words of spiritual comfort. And yet, throughout it all, he was not as he seemed. My initial reaction to this was naturally one of anger, as I believed that my trust had been betrayed in the very place where I believed it to be sacrosanct. I knew then how so many felt when they learned that their confessors, who had absolved their sins by day, were abusing children by night. But steadily I came to realize that no matter what sins he may have committed, my former confessor was still a Catholic cleric. This meant that what I confessed before him was, in reality, confessed to Christ. It was by reasoning thus that I eventually found the strength to forgive that priest, and to recover my inner peace.

My point in telling this story is simply to underline the fact, that while it is vital that a priest be rooted in Christ, it is ultimately Christ Himself who is revealed through the sacraments. The forgiveness that flows through the confessional, streams from the heart of the Redeemer, purging our impurities and salving our souls. It is He who, while looking down from the Cross, refuses to condemn our iniquities. Instead, He takes them upon Himself in an act of divine mercy. And so it is with all seven sacraments: from baptism to the Eucharist to the sacrament of holy orders, Christ is constantly giving of Himself for our deliverance.

This is why, when lived to the full, the Catholic life is replete with happiness. In baptism, we are given pride of place in the eternal community; in confession, we are forgiven even the most evil of acts; in confirmation, we receive the Holy Spirit as did the first apostles on the day of Pentecost; in the Eucharist, we are given Christ Himself to nourish and sustain the soul; in marriage, two people are gifted to each other in everlasting love; in the Sacrament of the Sick, we are anointed with the healing power of Christ; and in the Sacrament of Holy Orders, we are given the priesthood itself, as that through which all the other sacraments are made available.

Catholicism is, in other words, full of grace, which it constantly showers down upon all those seeking consolation. It feeds, forgives, confirms, unites, heals and saves. The sacraments are gifts which allow us to surmount the fallen or alienated condition. By authentically partaking of them, we are transported homewards and relieved of our earthly tribulations. But that, in turn, is not without its concrete consequences: you cannot lead a sacramental life without simultaneously becoming a better human being. When authentically lived, the sacraments cannot but transform a life in the image of Christ. That is why, as I have argued in previous chapters, the greatest of all sacraments – the Holy Eucharist – must be celebrated in sanctity and beauty. Otherwise, it fails to draw the parishioner into the mystery of Christ's living presence. It fails to convince that what is happening in its most sublime and sacred moments is a miracle, one whose purpose is to supply life eternal. Similarly, the other sacraments reveal Christ's healing and saving power. And when they are viewed with the eyes of faith, they have the power to literally re-make a person.

That is what my student experienced when he swapped the couch for the confessional: for the first time in his life, he understood what it meant to be *reborn* in Christ. And from that moment, he viewed the world and his neighbour, not merely as functional beings, but as gifts of creation. The gift which he had received changed his life to such an extent that he now viewed life itself as a gift, not to be used or abused, but to be treasured and loved.

It is in this context that Catholic teaching on sexuality should be situated. Catholicism does not deny that sexuality is fundamental to what we are as human beings. But it does hold that the primary purpose of human sexual desire is not pleasure. Its principal goal is the reciprocal love of another person. From the sacramental perspective, other people are not just a means to some further end, but are ends in themselves. They are not merely objects, but a revelation of the sacred. In a secular and sexualized culture, it is easy to forget that people are not simply flesh, but centres of selfhood. It is easy to think of them as purely physical beings devoid of a spiritual dimension. But not so when life is lived according to Catholic values, for it is impossible to view someone merely as a source of sexual pleasure while simultaneously conforming oneself to Christ in the sacraments. It is impossible to regard a person – *any* person - as a commodity or a thing when one's ethical paradigm demands that we love the neighbour as the self.

From the Catholic point of view, therefore, sex is an expression of one's love for another person, seen as a locus of sanctity. My desire is directed, not just at the body, but at *him* or *her* – this individual whose being the flesh contains. And that is why Catholics seek to sacramentalize their love in marriage. For them, marriage is more than just a verbal vow: it is a covenant to honour the dead and to prepare a place for the unborn. It is a promise to give the gift of life in honour of those who once gave it to us.

Put simply, there is no sphere of human life which the sacraments leave untouched. They are there for us at the beginning and at the end when existence is at its most fragile. They serve as a rite of passage into adulthood, and endow our sexual relations with a halo of holiness. They soothe us when we are sick, and nourish us in the midst of all our sorrow and joy. They permit us to live as if in the shadow of Christ: through them we can stand on Calvary, at the mouth of the empty tomb and in the upper room. And all the while, we become more Christ-like in our dealings with others, in as much as the sacramental is the natural enemy of selfishness. In Communion, I die to self in order to become one with Christ; in confession, I die to my old self in order to be reconciled to Christ; in marriage, I die to self in order to become one with another in a union consolidated by Christ; and through the sacrament of holy orders, I die to self in order to become another Christ.

To repeat, therefore, what I said in the last chapter: if genuine Catholic renewal is to become a reality, it will not be solely on the basis of parish councils, evangelization initiatives or ecumenical programmes, beneficial as all those things undoubtedly are. It will only happen when the sacramental life of local parishes can be revitalized, thus permitting His mercy to drop like the gentle rain of heaven upon the place beneath.

Conclusion

While writing this book, I appeared on an hour-long TV special entitled *Faith in Crisis*. Its purpose was to the future of Catholicism in the wake of the clerical child sex abuse crisis. My role on the programme was to advance the proposals for reform advanced in these chapters. It soon became clear, however, the show was ideologically driven in favour of the forces of rupture. The panel was loaded with disaffected clerics, disgruntled politicians, and even a woman who celebrates Mass each day in her home. We were also joined by three bishops who, from the outset, were aggressively assailed. One senior politician declared that she was 'shocked' at the sight of the Irish bishops kissing the Pope's ring during a recent crisis meeting with the Pontiff. Why, she asked, would grown men dress up in robes and act so 'obsequiously'. Alarmingly, the bishops had no answer to this, except to point out that it is protocol to wear a clerical cassock when meeting the Pope. What I expected them to say was something like: 'We kiss the Pope's ring because we believe he is Christ's vicar on earth.' I also expected them to point out that most Catholics not only greet the Pope by kissing his ring, but genuflect in the process. And they do so, not in order to be obsequious, but simply because they stand before St Peter's successor. But in the hostile environment of that TV studio, the bishops stayed silent in the face of fire.

During the course of the 'debate', I suggested that what Catholics must do is get back to basics through authentic participation in the Mass, which should be celebrated in holiness and beauty. Only then will both priest and parishioner rediscover the true power of the sacraments, whose intrinsic dignity and purity no amount of time or scandal can, or should compromise. Astonishingly, I was the only person on the panel to mention the sacraments or the Mass. But once I did, I too was attacked by the same contributors who had earlier sought to antagonize the bishops. At one point, I was interrupted by a liberal psychotherapist who shouted: 'We don't want that type of Catholicism!' I could only interpret this to mean that she wishes to dispense with the basic Catholic patrimony bequeathed to us by the first apostles. But the question which must then be asked is this: if your aim is to divest the faith of its timeless treasures, what type of Catholicism are you left with? The remainder of the programme supplied the answer: such people want a Church which is solely governed by 'the people'. They are not in pursuit of reform, but of a revolution in which the Catholic Hierarchy is dissolved in favour of democracy. They want bishops to be elected; they want lay people to possess the power to consecrate the sacred Host; they want all strictures on celibacy and sexuality to be removed. For them, liturgical and priestly reform is simply a side-issue. Their main objective is much more dramatic: it is to sever the link with the see of Peter, and thus with the ancient traditions of the Church which they consider to be 'totalitarian'. Inevitably, therefore, the programme descended into a clamour for the Pope's resignation, which, needless to say, the bishops refused to oppose.

Once aired, *Faith in Crisis* became a national talking-point in Ireland. Ordinary Catholics responded with dismay at the programme's blatant lack of balance, and at the failure of the bishops to adequately defend themselves, their leader and the doctrines of their faith. Others were incredulous that mention of the Mass was so aggressively dismissed, and that those who suggested that communion with Christ is the core of Catholicism, were instantly shut down. Judging by the public's reaction, it quickly became apparent that most of those on the panel did not represent the values and ideals of the great majority of Catholics – those for whom the sweet consolations of their faith remain sacrosanct, despite the horrors visited upon it by some terribly evil people. In essence, they were representative of a very vocal, but small minority for whom papal authority is the true cause of crisis within the Church. They belong, as such, to what George Weigel calls 'liberal Protestant Catholicism', a project which is blind to the fact that 'the liberal Protestant project is collapsing from its inherent theological incoherence'. Still, they constitute a powerful lobby-group in so far as they dominate university theology departments, and are favoured by the liberal media whenever it requires comment on Catholic issues. This conveys the impression that they speak on behalf of the world's Catholics, when in reality they speak for very few.

If there is one thing I have learned since the eruption of the clerical abuse crisis in Ireland, followed by that in Europe, is that ordinary Catholics desperately want their church to survive. Naturally, they want it cleansed of all iniquity and sin. But what they certainly do not want is for the abuse crisis to be used as a pretext to radically redefine the basic tenets of their faith. And that is so because they recognize that those tenets are not contingently grounded, but are the fruits of profound theological labour. What the Church gives its members is a sense of the everlasting in defiance of the temporal swirl. It enables them to connect with the great eternal society, to be at one with their dead and to commune directly with Christ. For them, the ancient rubrics and rituals of the old religion are not external or arbitrary embellishments, but the means by which Catholics can acquire a sense of their religious patrimony. This does not mean, of course, that certain features of church bureaucracy and clericalism do not frustrate them. But because they consider the core of Catholic life to be the sacraments, and because they regard the Mass as a miracle, they refuse to let church politics detract from that elemental experience of the Divine.

Put simply: the big problem with 'liberal Protestant Catholicism' is that it no longer believes in either the miracle of the Mass or the saving power of the sacraments. That is why, when I made mention of the Mass during the *Faith in Crisis* programme, I became the object of anger. To suggest that the key to Catholic reform is to rekindle the sanctity of the Eucharist, is considered by the forces of rupture as being too 'simplistic' an antidote. In reality, however, it is nothing of the sort. For what is Catholicism, if not the daily commemoration of Christ's death and resurrection? What is it, if not a belief in His real presence under the species of bread and wine? But once that is no longer believed, or once it is reduced to mindless monotony, then it does not matter what political initiatives are implemented. The core of the faith has been lost, and no amount of women priests or married clergy will succeed in reviving it. This brings me back once again to Monsignor Gilbey's belief that 'in order to put the world right, we must first establish the kingdom of God in our own hearts'. When the sacraments and the old devotions are no longer considered credible, it is then that Catholicism has become something else – something devoid of moral, theological and philosophical purpose. But when those ancient practices animate the life of a Catholic parish, people are inevitably revitalized in Christ. And in that moment, they cannot but become agents of charity, justice and love.

Still, the question persists: is it really plausible to say, in the wake of such a devastating crisis, that the Church will recover its soul through the Mass and the sacraments? Given, as I said at the outset, that the only connection most Catholics have to the Church is through the Mass, then it is surely reasonable to assume that if the Mass is properly celebrated it will do an enormous amount to sustain them in their faith. More importantly, when the Mass becomes the primary focus of a parish, when in other words parish life becomes Christ-centred, the potential for abuse, or indeed any form of evil, is infinitely diminished. But this, in turn, depends on people possessing a clear understanding of what it happening in the Mass. Hence the importance of catechesis in Catholic education, and why it needs to be enthusiastically imparted at an early age.

And to those who remain unconvinced by this, I simply point to the World Youth Day celebrations and to the enormous crowds that attend papal ceremonies in Rome and across the world. I point to all those parishes whose parishioners are in pain following the recent grim revelations, but who still cling to their faith because it is a source of hope in world where little exists. I point to groups like Communione e Liberazione (Communion and Liberation), whose Christian vibrancy inspires millions. Most especially, I point to all those small enclaves throughout the Catholic world where priests and parishioners gather weekly to consecrate themselves to Christ, and who do so with all the majesty and splendour which such a sacred event demands. Such people are the future of the Church, because they know that only where desecration has taken hold will scandal arise. Hence they reject rupture in favour of continuity, and in so doing are ever mindful of why beauty and sanctity are true paths to salvation.

In being purely politically motivated, 'liberal Protestant Catholicism' contends that you cannot have reform without revolution. And so, it seeks to extirpate all that it considers alien to its ultimate objective. This means 'deconstructing' any theology that blocks the revolutionary road. It is imperative when clearing a path to nowhere, in other words, that theology be divested of its transcendental or sacred dimension. For it is then that everything can be explained in purely temporal or scientific terms, thus permitting radical change where once it was forbidden. It is then that the Mass is considered meaningless – being, as one contributor to *Faith in Crisis* exclaimed, little more than 'magic'.

This type of thinking is, as I have suggested in this book, *anti-authoritarian*. It eschews anything which is not of this world, for to admit that there might be something beyond time and chance is to concede that we might be responsible to something greater than ourselves. That is why its archenemy is the humble prayer of gentle penitents in search of paradise. By aspiring heavenwards, such people are endeavouring, or so it is claimed, to give their beliefs an extraterrestrial backup which simply does not exist. In the mind of the neo-Darwinians and the postmodernists there is *only us*, perpetually severed from our heavenly origins. As everything is merely human, we have no need to prostrate ourselves before the Divine in docile obedience. For this is, in the words of philosopher Richard Rorty, the 'paradigm of subjection', one which should be replaced by 'a democratic culture' which prioritizes 'the duty to seek unforced agreement with other human beings about what beliefs will sustain and facilitate projects of social cooperation'.[1]

When viewed from that perspective, both the Mass and the sacraments do indeed resemble 'magic'. And when this outlook is promoted by people calling themselves 'Catholic'

---

1   Richard Rorty, 'Pragmatism as Anti-Authoritarianism' in *Revue Internationale de Philosophie*, Vol. 53, No. 207 (1/1999), p. 7.

you can be sure that they are nothing of the sort. Once again, their real objective is to undermine the claims to theological and moral authority exercised by the Pope and his bishops, thus opening the gates to liberal licence where once traditional values prevailed. In Chapter 2, I hinted at a possible rejoinder to this theology of estrangement. But there are some others, like Roger Scruton, who are also valiantly fighting in defence of what he calls 'the religious urge'.

In a piece entitled 'The Return of Religion', Scruton writes that modern people are drawn to religion 'by their consciousness of consciousness, by their awareness of a light shining in the centre of their being'. This suggests that human beings 'have an innate need to conceptualise their world in terms of the transcendental, and to live out the distinction between the sacred and the profane'. This need 'is rooted in self-consciousness and in the experiences that remind us of our shared and momentous destiny as members of Kant's "Kingdom of Ends".' Scruton believes, as do I, that 'religions satisfy this need', for they provide 'the social endorsement and the theological infrastructure that will hold the concepts of the transcendental and the sacred in place'.[2] To put it simply: the yearning for the sacred cannot be subdued, and Catholicism satisfies that yearning, not on the basis of political programmes, but by drawing its members to the mystery at the heart of creation. This is the ultimate mystery for all those who believe in the redeeming power of Jesus Christ, and for whom the sacraments are a source of love, sacrifice, forgiveness and beauty.

People who find meaning in the Mass are not deluded. Neither are they ignorant of science. If anything, they are

---

2   Roger Scruton, 'The Return of Religion' in Mark Dooley (ed.), *The Roger Scruton Reader* (London: Continuum, 2009), pp. 133–134.

pilgrims in that sphere which science cannot penetrate. There are, says Scruton, 'questions addressed to reason which are not addressed to science, since they are not asking for a causal explanation'. Such questions, like those regarding the intrinsic value of human life, animate the lives of Catholic believers. And it is not as though these people take their faith at face value, without any critical appraisal of its central claims. It is simply that having taken account of all opposing arguments, they follow Pope Benedict in concluding that unless 'there had been something extraordinary in what happened, unless the person and the words of Jesus radically surpassed the hopes and expectations of the time, there is no way to explain why he was crucified or why he made such an impact'. Isn't it reasonable to assume, in other words, that the Jesus of faith is not the product of a theology which was transplanted onto an historical individual after the fact, but 'that the greatness came at the beginning, and that the figure of Jesus really did explode all existing categories and could only be understood in the light of the mystery of God?'[3]

This, once again, is not to deny that much wrong has been done in the Church's name. My point is simply that through its sacramental life, and the divine energy which it supplies, the Catholic Church continues to offer a sense of home, belonging and enduring hope to millions across the globe. In the United States, for example, a prominent Jewish businessman Sam Miller, has taken up the Catholic cause because, as he says: 'There is a concerted effort by the media today to totally denigrate in every way the Catholic Church in this country.' Naturally, Miller is horrified at the

---

3   Pope Benedict XVI, *Jesus of Nazareth* Vol. 1 (London: Bloomsbury, 2007), pp. xxii–xxiii.

abuse scandal, solutions to which 'must be broader and deeper than those carried out by Catholic cardinals'. The whole church, he asserts, 'has a responsibility to offer decisive leadership in the area of sexual misconduct whether it is child abuse, sexual exploitation or sexual harassment'. He goes on to call for 'a broad based ecumenical council addressing the issue of sexual misconduct in the church, not only the Catholic Church, but all churches, including synagogues. Its goal would be transparency and openness in developing stringent, forward-looking guidelines, consistent with denominational distinctions, for preventing and addressing sexual misconduct within Christian churches and church-related institutions'.

Sam Miller believes that the Catholic Church has been hurt by 'an infinitesimally small number of wayward priests', which is why he sought to defend it in the course of a speech from 2003, the following portion of which is worth citing in full:

Do you know, and maybe some of you don't, the Catholic Church educates 2.6 million students everyday, at a cost to your Church of 10 billion dollars, and a savings on the other hand to the American taxpayer of 18 billion dollars. Needless to say, Catholic education at this time stands head and shoulders above every other form of education that we have in this country [the United States]. And the cost is approximately 30% less. If you look at our own Cleveland school system, they can boast of an average graduation rate of 36%. Do you know what it costs you and me as far as the other 64% who didn't make it? Look at your own records. You (Catholic schools) graduate 89% of your students. Your graduates in turn go on to graduate studies at the rate of 92%, and all at a cost to you. To the rest of the Americans it's free, but it costs you Catholics at least 30% less to educate students compared to the costs that the public education system pays out for education that cannot compare. Why? Why would these enemies of the Church try to destroy an institution that has 230 colleges and universities in the United States with an enrolment of 700,000 students? Why would anyone want to destroy an institution like the Catholic Church which has a non-profit hospital system of 637 hospitals which account for hospital treatment of 1 out of every 5 people not just Catholics in the United States today? Why would anyone want to destroy an institution like that? Why would anyone want to destroy an institution that clothes and feeds and houses the indigent – 1 of 5 indigents in the United States? I've been to many of your shelters and no one asks them if you are a Catholic, a Protestant or a Jew; just 'come, be fed, here's a sweater for you and a place to sleep at night' at a cost to the Church of 2.3 billion dollars a year. The Catholic Church today has 64 million members in the United States and is the largest non-governmental agency in the country. It has 20,000 churches in this country alone. Every year they raise approximately $10 billion to help support these agencies.[4]

It is regrettable that the Catholic hierarchy does not highlight such facts more often in its own defence. They stand, nevertheless, as an indisputable testimony to the Church's truly potent power for good. And the same is true wherever and whenever the Catholic Church implants its

---

4   Speech delivered by Sam Miller, City Club of Cleveland (6 March 2003), and published in the *Buckeye Bulletin* (May-June, 2003).

ancient roots. That is why, rather than falling prey to misery and despair, Catholics should focus instead on the glorious achievements of their faith. Only then will they see that the real antidote to the Church's problems lies not in rupture or revolution, but in those sacramental wonders which continue to constitute humanity's greatest hope.